# IRRESISTIBLE HUSBAND

## For the Man Who Wants to Know ...

*Edwin Louis Cole*

watercolor books™

**Southlake, Texas**

*IRRESISTIBLE HUSBAND: For the Man Who Wants to Know ...*

ISBN 1-929496-08-7
Copyright © 2001 by Edwin Louis Cole
Christian Men's Network
P. O. Box 10
Grapevine, Texas 76099

Published by Watercolor Books
P. O. Box 93234
Southlake, TX 76092
www.watercolorbooks.com

Cover painting by Lyn Conlan
www.watercolorlyn.com

To Nancy,

again and always

# TABLE OF CONTENTS

# INTRODUCTION

This book is written for the man who has seen divorce become acceptable, but doesn't want it for himself—for the man who wants to enjoy marriage throughout life instead of enduring it for the children's sake—for the man who wants to overcome the compromise of previous generations, parents, and politicians, to become the best he can be in every way. It's for the man who wants to know what his father failed to teach him, what women couldn't tell him, and what his pastor wanted to say, but only behind closed doors. This is written for the man who wants to be known as a mature man, a real man, a man who "knows."

This is for the man who fears, has failed, or is faltering at marriage, and for the man who is launching into marriage for the first time. It's for the young man who is wondering if he's ready, or if he's found the "right" woman, or is preparing himself for her. And it's for the married man who thinks he might be able to do better. More than anything, this book is written for the man who wants to succeed in everything he tries, including relationships.

## A NEW GENERATION OF LEADERS

This is also for the new generation of family leaders who learned about women from Daisy Duke, Madonna or *Baywatch* and have since discovered that wasn't education enough. It is for the man who learned about relationships from music videos or after-school television specials—learned nutrition from Happy Meals® and Little Debbie® snacks—learned character from the Hardy Boys, Cosby or the Muppets—learned to read from *Sesame Street*—learned fashion by wearing Bugle Boys or a sequinned glove—learned strategy by playing army men—who saw a president shot or a space shuttle explode, but whose scars are from skateboards and in-line skates—who learned to escape by building a fort or through Saturday morning episodes of *Scooby-Doo* or *Thunder Cats*, and who may still escape by watching Cartoon Network® or taking off for Florida.

This is written for the man who has tried Coke®, New Coke®, Coke Classic®, or even cocaine, but whose true goal is to find the "real thing." For the man who doesn't care if he came from Venus or Mars, a stork or a pumpkin patch, but wants to learn the truth about himself, and what he can do to create fulfilling, lasting relationships with his wife and children.

And this book is written in love, because *love is the qualification to speak the truth*. As a man who was married to the same lovely lady for more than a half century, my prayer is that the truths in the following pages will make a vital difference in whatever you call "home."

WE ARE MEN! When we are fulfilled in our manhood, our truths, role models, and foundations for living don't come from television or mystery stories, but from one source alone—the written Word of God, the Bible. God the Creator is the Divine Coach Who alone knows what we were created to be and become. He is the official guide to becoming truly manly.

If you are looking for a simple list of things to do, you won't find it as such in this book. Yes, there are lists, but God's will cannot be contained in or limited by lists. If you are looking for a quick fix, a way to get your wife to change, or a method to avoid the consequences of poor decisions, you will be disappointed in the following pages.

But if you are a man who wants to live life to the full, who wants to build an indestructible marriage—a man who is willing to face reality and take a hard look at yourself from the inside-out—then you're the best reader for this book. You are a man on the way to a new level of living, and a candidate for becoming an irresistible husband.

## You Will Gain New Weapons

"The weapons of our warfare are not carnal, but mighty through God to the pulling down of strongholds ..."[1]

Life exists beyond army men, guns, footballs, remote controls or bigger wheels. God gives men real weapons we need to fight the battles we face in life.

Moses had a rod and fed the people with God's heavenly manna. Samson won with the jawbone of an ass. Elijah passed on a mantle. Streaked rods gained Jacob his fortune and God created a ladder to show him the way to heaven. David made a slingshot to launch a smooth stone that killed Goliath. Jesus used His own saliva to make a mud ball that healed the blind.

God uses the "foolish things to confound the wise." You already have what God can use to do what God wants to do without trying to get anything else.

You don't need caviar or Happy Meals®—just manna from heaven, the "bread of life," to overcome a wilderness experience. That's where God's provision is.

You don't need whitewater rafting or the Jungle Cruise at *Disneyland*—just the "washing in the water of the Word" to escape to the Promised Land. That's where God's power is.

You don't need a fort, castle, or cathedral—just a tabernacle in the wilderness to worship God. That's where God's friendship is.

You don't need a silver-tongued sense of humor or new dance moves—just the anointing to speak God's words. That's where God's creativity is.

You don't need to become the owner of a "dotcom," nor be the best in your profession—just become a "living stone" fitly joined in worship. That's where God's glory is.

You don't need red *Kool Aid* or Little Debbie® snacks—just the bread and wine of communion. That's where God's covenant is.

You don't need entertainment or *Nickelodeon*—just the Word of God undiluted. That's where God's wisdom is.

You don't need *Sesame Street, Rolling Stone* or *Esquire*—just knowledge and truth, light and life. That's where God's integrity is.

As you read this book, you will gain new weapons and skills for knowing both the will and the way of God, so you can live with the power of God's presence in your life. Israel knew the *works* of God, but Moses knew His *ways*. Likewise, *the man who knows* how *will always have a job, but the man who knows* why *will always be his boss.*

In marriage, the man who knows *what* is happening in his family will live on one level, but the man who knows *why* will always have the edge.

We are men!

This book is not for the curious, nor for shelf material, nor a reference for arguments. This book is for the one who genuinely wants to be more than a mere male, who has an inkling or perhaps a passion to discover more about manhood than what the world has taught, and who believes he may have the makings of becoming a real man and an irresistible husband. To that man I say, may God grant you your heart's desire!

[1] II Corinthians 10:4

# Chapter One

# Culture is the Culprit

It's not all your fault.

That's good news, and probably the last thing you expected to read. You no doubt picked up this book because you felt responsible for being a husband. You may have assumed you had some hard lessons to learn in order to nurture your wife's love or build a marriage that lasts.

The truth is, if your relationship is not the best, it is not all your fault. But it is equally true that you'll have to learn some lessons to create a lasting relationship, because ultimately you are responsible before God as a steward of that marriage. If you choose to read the rest of this book, you will become fully responsible for what it says. So already, right up front, you have to ask, *Am I man enough to read beyond the first page?*

We are men. We're not angels. We're not computers or machines. We're not supermen or action heroes or champions of the universe. We're just men. And we were placed on this earth by God as stewards of His creation. All He expects of us is to be men. He knows the struggles we encounter to achieve manhood, to be real men, especially in relationship to a woman—the hardships we face as we become an "irresistible husband."

A great part of our fight today for our manhood and for our marriage arises from the culture in which we live. Culture is composed of customs, traditions, art, music, language, literature and institutions. Our culture is marked by a steady spread of immoral behavior that weakens family life, promotes disrespect for authority, and insults the practice of personal responsibility. In our worldwide community, civilization as we know it, culture is culprit.

## Jesus Taught About Culture

Two parables taught by Jesus Christ explain this. In the "Parable of the Prodigal Son," Jesus draws a word picture of humanity. Jesus said a prodigal son asked his father for his inheritance, then squandered it in a foreign place. He ended up working in the stench of a pigsty for a Gentile, the lowest level for a nice Jewish boy, until he returned to his right mind and to his father's house. After suffering the hunger pangs of near-starvation, upon his return, the father welcomed the son with joy and feasting.

The interesting part of that story is that it wasn't the devil that caused the prodigal to leave the "Father's house." Satan is nowhere in that story. The young man himself just wanted to get out, take the money and run, and live life to the fullest. Why? In contradiction to the government of his father's house, the attraction of the culture with all it had to offer lured the son away. Believing he was missing some of the best things in life, the prodigal left home to enjoy and spend his money on all that culture had to offer. He found that what it offered was empty, vain, and vapid. The son did not know the difference between liberty and license until he had left the father, squandered his inheritance on "riotous living" (partying), and found himself alone, at his wits' end, working in a pigsty, suffering from famine. When your so-called friends are unavailable in your darkest hour and the finest thing you can find to eat is an empty pea pod, you are existing, not really living.

In the Lord's parable of the "Seed and the Sower," we see the truth in another way. A farmer spreads good seed, but once the seed is sown, it is not up to the seed to produce. It is up to the soil to make the seed produce. The condition of the soil determines the destiny of the seed. Jesus discusses four kinds of soil on which the farmer's seeds are sown, as illustrations of the seed of God's Word sown in our hearts.

The first seed is sown, and immediately birds come and snatch it away. This illustrates that the Word is sown, but Satan immediately destroys the Word by planting doubts or sending a contradictory "false" word to keep that seed from germinating. These "false words" are lies spread through the culture.

The second seed is sown on stony ground. The seed springs up, but because of its shallow roots, it cannot withstand the heat of the day. Jesus is saying that the Word sown causes immediate gladness, but no real root can form because of the hard areas in the heart. When affliction or persecution come, those with stony hearts stumble and fall away.

The third seed is sown in thorny soil which chokes it out before it can really get started. The cares and anxieties of the world, the distractions of the age, the pleasure, delight, false glamour, deceitfulness of riches, and the craving and passionate desire for other things creep in to choke the Word and it dies.

The fourth seed is sown on good soil and produces at the rate of thirtyfold, sixtyfold, or a hundredfold, yielding a huge crop for the farmer.

Let's understand this parable. Twenty-five percent of the crop grew on good soil. Another twenty-five percent was stolen or damaged by the devil. But the second and third seeds—a full fifty percent of the crop—were damaged by the culture of the day. The culture was the culprit.

## THE BATTLEGROUND IS THE CULTURE

Much of our battleground today is in our own culture. In both parables, the culture of the day seduced, enticed, drew away, corrupted, pressured and ruined man and seed. Culture undermines manhood, causing men to adapt to the world and die from it, rather than overcoming and subduing it. Too many Christian men spend one hundred percent of their time fighting the devil, which is only twenty-five percent of the problem, rather than dealing with the culture into which they've been born.

When God sent the children of Israel into Canaan, seven nations lived there. All seven were heathen idolaters, practicing a culture that was antagonistic to the manner in which God wanted Israel to live. The children of Israel were told to occupy the land by conquering those enemies. God knew that if the idolatrous nations stayed in the land, Israel would be seduced by their culture. So, in a "scorched earth" policy, God gave instructions to destroy utterly the old culture, lest they be destroyed by it.

The Israelites under Joshua's leadership started out doing exactly as God said, destroying cultures, subduing their enemies, ensuring the world around them conformed to their ideals and standards, rather than them conforming to the traditions of the world into which they were thrust. Then Joshua died and "there arose a new generation which knew not the Lord."[1] That generation began to adapt to the ways of the world, worshiping the Baals and Ashtoreth, offering their children in the fire of Molech, and sinning against God. The new generation chose to ignore the warning God had given their fathers, and adopted the ways of the culture around them. As a result, the Israelites suffered at the hands of their enemies, becoming slaves to those whom they were supposed to conquer, and God became their adversary instead of their friend.

Today you and I find ourselves in a similar situation. We are surrounded by a culture that teaches lying even in leadership, allows lawlessness, and gives license to do anything rather than liberty to do the right thing. Into such an age you were born, and into such a culture you are trying to carve a place for you, your wife and your children to live.

Divorce in our culture is no longer just an option. It is an expectation. In a bygone era, divorce was considered a scandal, something from which a man could scarcely recover. Divorce would affect his career, his ability to run for public office, his leadership in the community, and would call into question his judgment wherever he went. Yet it is now so normal as to be a non-issue. That is, a non-issue for everyone except the family ravaged by the pain and mistrust divorce always brings. Yet even the heartbreak of broken relationships has become an expectation and is treated as sport and entertainment. Movies depict it, talk shows legitimize it, and "real-TV" programs exploit it. *Culture is the culprit.*

Seduced into believing people can do "their thing" without thought or concern about others, softened by the bending of beliefs which were once rock solid, silenced by our own confusion as to what we should stand up for and what we should allow to slide, we muck around in a miry mess trying to move toward the one we love, raising a muddied arm here or a murky leg there and wonder why-oh-why is this relationship so hard?

I was raised not far from the La Brea tar pits of Los Angeles, which are like giant mud puddles except they are filled with a natural, steaming tar that has an odor so strong it can be smelled upon approach, long before it is seen. Today the pits are protected by a fence and surrounded with a park-like setting, but in my boyhood they were simply a place to play, where we would throw things just to watch them get sucked into the bubbling tar. It was sport to us, to play with these dangerous pits that had subdued prehistoric animals many times larger than any of us, long before our time. Today's culture reminds me of those pits. Stinky, dangerous, oozing, ready for its next victim, yet treated as a plaything by boys and girls alike who call themselves "adults."

## THE CULTURE OF CHRISTIANITY

We are born naturally into the culture of our country. But when we are born again spiritually, we are born anew into the culture of Christianity. We are no longer subject to the sticky ooze of the natural culture, which can suck us in and destroy us. We are no longer held captive to the culture around us, but we can apprehend that for which we were apprehended.[2] We can aspire to and attain a higher level of life than the culture in which we've been born. Why settle for less than that for which Christ died?

I was in another country preparing to preach when I determined the Spirit of the Lord would have me speak about sex sins to the merged congregations gathered there. Returning to the break room after the message, I noticed a total silence among the pastors. After a few minutes I queried aloud as to the reason for the silence. Finally, one of the brethren spoke up and said, "We do not speak of that among our people, because we feel that promiscuity is just part of our culture."

Is promiscuity a part of the culture of Christianity? That's impossible, according to Scripture. Yet it appears that promiscuity is as much a part of church life as the life of the unchurched. Why? Because through our silence, we have adopted the traits of the culture around us. *A man's silence lets the devil shout. When Christians speak, the devil is silent.*

Another time, I was in Uganda speaking about manhood, which included a teaching about sexual intimacy. The church in which I spoke was overrun with people. They sat on the floors, filled the aisles, pressed themselves through windows from the outside, and had speakers outdoors for those who were unable to squeeze in. All that was left for me was about a three-foot circle from which to speak. Although they must have been uncomfortable, the people sat in rapt attention, not moving lest they miss even a word of the message. We must have held our positions there for two hours, as the Holy Spirit encouraged me how to minister to these eager, listening hearts.

When it was over, one of my associates explained the behavior of one pastor on the front row of this jam-packed, overcrowded, stuffy building, who seemed to suffer the whole time I spoke. My associate said this was the same pastor who had refused to allow him to mention the word "sex" in his church on the previous Sunday. "We don't talk about things like this to our people," the pastor had explained.

There we were, in a country where 33% of the population is dying from the AIDS virus, where families and genealogies have been stopped dead by the disease, and where the streets continue to fill with orphaned children—and the pastor refuses to mention the word "sex" to his people! "Like priest, like people," the scripture says.[3]

Think of the deaths in Africa that could have been prevented if ministers from a previous era had taught the truth about sexual intimacy in the Christian culture, instead of encouraging people to be mute on the topic and subject to their sexually promiscuous culture. *Silence was the structure in which ignorance caused disease and death to reign.*

## A "SCORCHED-EARTH" POLICY

We live in a culture of sexual leniency, and sexually transmitted disease. We live in a culture of loosed-from-restraint living, which is the definition of "lasciviousness," talked about in the Bible. We live in a culture that promotes heartache in child and adult alike. We live in a culture without trust, without intimacy, without openness, and by and large, without love. We live in a culture of "no-fault" divorce.

Jehovah God knew His people could be seduced by their fleshly natures to adopt the practices of unbelievers in the culture around them. His "scorched earth" policy was intended to eliminate the temptation and free His people to live under His divine blessing. We need a "scorched earth" policy for ourselves as well, to build a strong and lasting marriage and see God's hand upon our lives and the lives of our families.

It doesn't matter the culture you name—whether contending against persecution in a Muslim nation, or contending for the faith in a formerly Christian culture that is undergoing a cultural shift—we must all be men who are MEN! Men who don't float with the current, but make decisions, hold convictions, admit when we're wrong, face harsh realities, and admit our own need when necessary as we battle our way upstream culturally.

The culture of Christianity is an international, intertribal, interracial culture. It has nothing to do with ethnic type, and everything to do with blood type—for those of us who have the Blood of Jesus as a covering for our sins.

Jesus hung on the cross between two thieves. One thief slandered Jesus, railing against him with the fury the crowd had shown in demanding Christ's crucifixion. That thief lived by the standards of the day's culture, and died by the same. The other thief broke with the old culture and confessed his belief in Christ. One died to live in eternal perdition, the other died on earth but found himself instantly in Paradise to live eternally with the Lord.

Today men have the choice to live by the culture of the day or to receive the authority of the Word of God and the ability of the Spirit of God that enables us to live in a new culture based on God's moral law of love.

When the Prodigal Son returned home, destroyed from living in the world's culture, his father's grace was shown by the bounty of forgiveness and restoration he offered. We see this grace and mercy echoed in the words of Jesus when a woman was taken in by the adultery of her culture yet to whom Jesus said, "Neither do I condemn thee—go and sin no more."[4] This is what Jesus would say to us today when we're caught in the snares of our culture.

Jesus' story of the prodigal son shows that we are all "prodigals" at best and must return to the "Father's House." The difference between the "prodigal" and many men today is that the prodigal was raised in the "father's house," so he knew where to go when he needed help. Men who have never been raised in church, or in a good home, have no understanding of how to find God, or the "Father's House." They need someone to help them find their way. If that's you, this book is your pathway to His home.

This book is intended to lead you through the muck and mire of our own culture, on a road to finding an indestructible marriage, a superhighway to take you to the point of becoming an "irresistible husband." If you're willing to adopt a "scorched earth" policy, to accept responsibility for your marriage and for the lessons in this book, then I can guarantee you an increase in the stature and measure of your manhood, and a newfound respect from yourself as well as those around you. You're a man. You can be even more of a man today!

[1] Judges 2:10
[2] Philippians 3:12
[3] Hosea 4:9
[4] John 8:11

# Chapter Two

# Make a Decision

The problem with many men is that they marry, then attempt to continue living as a single. It never works.

*Decisions determine conduct, character and destiny.* "Location, location, location" is the formula for success in business. "Decision, decision, decision" is the formula for success in life. No decision is a decision by default. Indecision is still a decision—it's just a decision not to decide.

Deciding to marry is one of the two greatest decisions you will ever make in your life. When a man decides to marry, he generally buys the ring, books the honeymoon, packs his bag, moves into a new apartment, and thinks he's done his part. Wrong. There's much, much more to deciding on marriage than packing a bag, taking a trip, buying a ring or moving furniture. You're not really living as a married man until you decide, once and for all, that you're married—and that it is for life. Married men who try to live as though they are single, are miserable men. Torn between two lifestyles—and the demands of each—they waiver, and in their "double-minded" thoughts, become unstable in every way.

I've jokingly said, "Marriage is a great institution—if you like institutions." Men who make right decisions find great freedom in marriage. Those who don't, find marriage confining. Marriage holds tremendous freedoms—never worrying about a date for Friday night, freedom from celibacy, freedom to become completely yourself and build a new life apart from your birth family.

The adult world is a world of decision-making. Many men are frustrated because of their own ineptness at making decisions. They demand to be called "men," yet their decisions reveal the weaknesses in their own characters. Lashing out at others, they hinder their own development by making decisions emotionally, or by refusing to decide.

Decide to be married! Act married. Live married. If you're just now planning to be married, you are at ground zero. Learn. Build. Develop.

When you decide to marry, you decide as well to rise to the occasion and acquire the necessary maturity, or you'll immediately start to fail. Like a rocket that falls over on the launch pad, you may have a sizzling wedding and honeymoon, but you'll have to begin maturing immediately if you want those rocket launchers actually to get you off the ground. You must first learn to treat your wife as a wife, not as one of the guys, and certainly not as a "mom." At men's seminars conducted by our ministry, we hold a "graduation" where each of the men reduces his life's mission into a one-sentence declaration. At one of them, one man took the mike and bellowed, "Good bye Mom, hello wife!"

When we're young, our mothers do two things for us: they correct us, and make our decisions for us. But as adults, we make our own decisions and are free from dependence upon parents. The problem with many men is, once they marry, they refuse to make decisions, or refuse to decide wisely. This means their wives correct them and make decisions for them, which turns their wives into their mothers. I call such a man an *adult adolescent.*

A child is the center of his own universe, throws tantrums, is insensitive to others' needs, demands his own way, is unable to be reasoned with, acts irresponsibly, and only responds to concrete authority. This is the state of many married men today. Only when they see their clothes strewn across the front lawn or have divorce papers served do they accept the demand to grow up.

When a man makes his wife act like his mother, he creates more than just a maturity crisis, because he cannot make love to his mother. Due to the man's immaturity, the entire relationship suffers, then he blames her for not satisfying his "needs."

Men can prolong adolescence. We're only young once, but we can live immature for a lifetime.

*Maturity does not come with age but begins with the acceptance of responsibility.* Those without maturity find their way difficult and frustrating. Those with it find their way easy and satisfying.

## Start Making Good Decisions

Good decision-making is an acquired art, which has maturity as its foundation. Years ago in Old Testament days, Abraham made a decision by default. When his wife, Sarah, suggested they could have a child if he would sleep with Hagar, her assistant, Abraham went along with the plan. The child he had with Hagar was Ishmael, the father of the far-flung Arab nations. Abraham repented for not waiting on God, and Sarah finally became pregnant with the child God had promised them. She gave birth to Isaac, the father of today's Jewish nation. From birth, Ishmael was hostile toward Isaac. The resulting acrimony and war between the two peoples exists right up to the present day.

Often the stress we find in our lives stems from our own poor decisions. We make an "Ishmael" decision, then wonder why we can't just enjoy the "Isaac" decision we also made. Each day of our lives builds upon the day before, which built upon the day before that. Poor decisions today bring friction and distress into our tomorrows. *Poor decisions ruin destinies, and frustrate the fulfillment of God's purposes for our lives.*

A young man I know named Bryan is living proof. Bryan knows the truth and can say it when he is drunk, but can't admit it when he's sober. Married, attending church, helping others, with a great job and a beautiful wife, Bryan had it all. But he became unhappy with his marriage when his daughter was born. Until then, his wife had been a steady date, someone beautiful to dangle from his arm. But with the added responsibility of a child, she didn't seem fun anymore. He enjoyed carnal pleasures with his work associates and indulged his every whim, while ignoring the Word of God and his marriage. Ignorant of the Lord's teaching, he was devoid of God's character.

Bryan tried to serve both God and the worldly pleasures his money could afford. His failure to make a basic decision between the two led to frustration which he assuaged by entering into an extra-marital affair. When he was caught, rather than restoring his relationship with his wife, he turned to other women. The girlfriend who bore his second child was not even someone he liked. But by then he was estranged from the wife of his youth and their child, living with the girlfriend, drinking to escape his pain, and Bryan's once vibrant life had become a quagmire of confusion and guilt.

Bound by denial, Bryan makes wrong decisions because he has never made the first, basic decision of manhood—to admit his need for God. Bryan now serves gods he created to avoid submitting to the Creator God—gods of materialism, pleasure, and escapism. *Manmade gods always degrade us. The one true God always works for our highest good.*

In the Lord's parable of the prodigal, He taught that when a decision is made to love God with our whole hearts, all else begins to fall into place and our lives change for the better. In much the same way, many husbands take a wife's love and squander it. Then, when she doesn't love him anymore, he wonders what happened. God is forgiving. Many wives aren't.

Winning back a wife who has been hurt is one of the hardest efforts a man will ever make. That's why I teach that "*new construction is always easier than reconstruction.*" Better to make right decisions—to love God and love your wife—the first time around.

## CHRISTIANITY OR CHURCHIANITY?

Those who have been raised in church often face another drawback. They can become church-wise, just as men on the streets become street-wise. They can know the truth, but through cynicism and unbelief, not allow it to set them free. "*Churchianity" is growing up in church. Christianity is growing up in Christ.* The two can be as far apart as heaven and hell.

Kong was nineteen years old, an all-star water polo member of Singapore's army team, when he heard the truth that "*manhood and Christlikeness are synonymous.*" That day, without hesitation, he made a decision to be a man who "maximized" his manhood by becoming like Christ. Kong's love for Jesus, His Savior and Lord, became his passion in life. The merchants of his nation worship the dollar, and traditional Asians worship religions with idols, but Kong became a disciple, not just a convert, of Christ. Kong made a good decision. He realized what many men fail to see: that financial success on earth cannot help a man avoid the wrath of God when he leaves this earth.

In the time of Jesus, some people equated financial prosperity with being truly religious. Even today, some think the mark of a true believer is financial success. Jesus told a parable about Lazarus, who was a beggar in this life, and a rich man named Dives, who became a beggar in eternity. Dives, the rich man, was a child of wrath and an heir of hell who had feasted sumptuously in his house before his death. Lazarus, a child of love and an heir of heaven lay at Dives' gate, smelling the scents of rich foods that wafted from Dives' kitchen, yet perishing for hunger.

Both men died. For Lazarus, the beggar, his body was tumbled into an unmarked, indigent's grave, the same burial as an ass. The rich man had a pompous funeral, lay in state, with mourners and a cortege of what would be considered in those days limousines which followed his body to the graveside. Standing by the monument at his grave was a priest and friends who praised him. Paid mourners gave homage with much weeping.

The difference between the two men on earth was nothing to compare with the difference after they died. Lazarus' body lay in a pauper's unmarked grave, but his spirit was carried by angels into the bosom of Abraham, the "father of the faithful," in Heaven. Jesus said the rich man, in utmost anguish at the torment of hell, lifted up his eyes and saw Abraham and Lazarus. His misery was compounded by seeing the happiness of Lazarus. The same Lazarus whom he had disregarded, considered a nuisance, and unworthy of anything but crumbs, he now saw in preferential seating.

Dives shouted in agony, "Have mercy on me." He desired just a drop of water to cool his tongue, the same tongue that scorned and ridiculed Lazarus as he lay at Dives' gate. Dives now saw the consequences of ignoring truth. He realized too late an enormous gulf was fixed between him and Lazarus, and nothing could be done to change it.

Heaven is comfort. Hell is torment. Heaven is laughter and joy unspeakable. Hell is weeping and pain excruciating. Heaven is a place of love, and hell a place of lust. Love is easily satisfied. Lust is insatiable. Hell's torment, in part, is never finding or having even a moment of satisfaction, comfort, love or forgiveness.

Dives, the rich man in Hell, pleaded with Abraham, "Send Lazarus back to my house. Let him tell my brothers what condition I am in. Let him warn them not to go on living like I taught them, lest they also come into this place of torment." Dives was the beggar now. Having been indifferent to the message of eternal life, content with his temporal and material lifestyle, he would now give anything to be able to do it over. For the first time, he thinks of his brothers and begs on their behalf. But *no request is granted in hell.*

The kindest saint in heaven cannot visit the congregation of the dead and damned, to comfort or relieve any who were once their friends. The most daring sinner in hell cannot force his way out of that prison, cannot get over that gulf, cannot bridge the gap, cannot escape from the eternal consequence of his failure to make the right decision.[1] Death has no favorites. Disease knows no stranger.

God had already given Dives and his brothers the testimony of Moses and the prophets, the means of conviction and conversion. They had the written word. They had the church. Each had the testimony of his own conscience. Abraham in essence told Dives, "Your brothers have the gospel, the Word of the Lord, and those who preach it. Let them listen and believe. If they don't hear Moses and the prophets, neither will they be persuaded even if one rises from the dead." They went to church, but never believed. A messenger from the dead can say no more than what is said in the scriptures, nor say it with more authority.

Your first basic choice involves your last actions before eternity. Limousines or angels will carry you out. Your eternal destiny is determined by your decision in this life. There is no second chance to live today or tomorrow. Today is the day of decision. To love God or not to love God—that is the question. What's your final answer?

## THE CLOSEST THING TO HEAVEN OR HELL

We can have a foretaste of eternity in this life. After choosing to love God and place Him first, marriage is the second greatest decision we'll ever make. It can be the closest thing to heaven or hell that we will ever know on this earth. Contrast the failure of Bryan and the success of Kong in the elementary decision they made, and its consequences.

Kong cemented his decision to live for God by making the godly of the land his heroes rather than the ungodly, and he fueled his appetite to learn the Word of God with passionate obedience.[2] As he did, Kong grew in favor with both God and man. He developed a following of young people whom he sparked with a flame of heaven-bent desire which eventually grew into a church.

At the beginning, Kong took a vow of purity, determining not to date for five years. As the years came to a close, a trusted advisor told him to make a decision about marriage—that day! The only person Kong could imagine marrying was Sun, the beautiful worship leader at the growing church he had started. Hearing the voice of the Lord through his mentor, immediately Kong went to Sun's office, knocked on the door, and proposed marriage. She accepted.

Kong's is a marriage authored by heaven. Sun is an absolutely beautiful and godly woman of immense talent and dedication to the Lord that matches his. Blessed, serving God together, living their dream, Kong and Sun are a unique pair of godly young people who are enjoying the reward and fruit of righteous decisions.

Kong's initial decision was strengthened each day as he continued to stick with his commitment to Christ. Kong's life proves *the only scripture we really believe is the one we obey.* Kong obeyed.

## Your Power Is In Your Choices

What a difference between Bryan and Kong. Two men almost the same age, having the same talents and opportunities, knowing the same God, but with different decisions and a far different destiny. Both are making an enormous difference in the lives of family, friends and others around them, but with a far different result. One is suffering the consequences of his decision, the other is enjoying the reward. One has caused a rift that will make his daughter and ex-wife suffer for years to come. The other has caused a union that produces joy in his own life and inspires everyone around him to do the same.

All sin is a form of insanity. *Sin always promises to please and serve, but only desires to enslave and dominate.*

Men who think they live "free" from God are in chains to the bondage of sin. The freedom of marriage is freedom from sexually-transmitted diseases, from heartbreak, from unwanted pregnancies, from courtrooms, from garnished wages, from child-sharing on weekends and holidays. When married men choose not to be or act married, they trade their freedoms for bondages of lies, adultery, guilt, condemnation, confused children, and broken hearts.

A great man once said, "Whatever you look to for the solution to your problems becomes your god." Alcohol is one of Bryan's gods because he finds escape from his conscience in the bottle. Denial is another god, avoiding truth as if avoidance alone offers a solution to problems. Denial is the refusal to acknowledge or believe something real. Men live in denial when they refuse to accept responsibility for their own actions. Their denial serves as a barrier to prevent help, cure or deliverance.

Make a decision today!

The Bible says we as men are given the power of choice. Free will separates humans from animals. God brought us into the world so we could choose Him. *Once we make a choice, however, we become the servant to that choice.* Choose avoiding, covering up, lying or escaping, and we'll become the servant of the same—working hard to avoid, cover up, lie and escape. Choose responsibility, making right decisions, and becoming a trustworthy man, and we'll become the servant to our good decisions and the recipient of trust. It's all within our power. Our choice.

The first major decision men must make is to follow after the Lord Jesus Christ and allow Him to live His life through us. The second decision is to take a wife. The first decision will take us to a literal Heaven or Hell. The second decision will take us to the next closest thing to heaven or hell on this earth.

*Life is composed of our choices and constructed by our words.* If you want to change your life, change your choices and your words. Choices determine conduct, character and destiny. Choices are based on what you believe, and what you believe about God, yourself, your wife, and others has the greatest potential for good or harm in your life.

When God said, "You shall have no other gods before me," He meant exactly that.

Your first basic choice will give you limousines now or angels later. Your second choice, to marry for life, will keep you off the slippery slope that ends in destruction.

[1] Henry, Matthew. *Commentary on the Holy Bible.* Philadelphia: Lippincott, 1856.
[2] Psalm 16:3 TLB; Psalm 101:6 TLB

## CHAPTER THREE

## AVOID THE EASY TRAPS

If a man can be deceived, he can be conquered.

The pattern is deception—denial—distraction—dislocation—destruction. You can be deceived if you can be convinced to deny reality. Once you are deceived and distracted, you can be dislocated from the original path on which you started. Diverted to the wrong path, destruction is just a matter of time.

To reach your goals as a man and as a husband, you have to avoid these obvious mistakes. Satan comes to steal, kill and destroy.[1] But he never shows himself as a "messenger of evil," as you see in movies. He always appears as an "angel of light," making temptations appear normal and desirable. Even obviously bad decisions can seem logical, reasonable and sometimes profitable. Satan has made pornography and adultery seem harmless and mainstream, as if "everybody's doing it" so it must be okay. In reality, such deception is sent to destroy men, marriages and children.

### STAY AWAY FROM PLAGUES!

One of our ministry teams went to Romania to plant men's ministry in that formerly Communist nation. A grown Romanian orphan named Dorel, who had experienced painful rejection and abandonment throughout most of his life, hit on the irony of their mission. "After America sent us drugs, pornography, and homosexuality," Dorel said, "it is only right that they would bring a ministry now to teach us how to be real men."

Two pandemic problems cover the planet and can be found in almost every culture: Fatherlessness and pornography. Each wreaks havoc because of the men they mold. One produces men who were never taught to be men, the other produces men who refuse to be.

Some choices are so evident, the difference between right and wrong so apparent, it seems implausible that a man could make the wrong decision and fall into a trap. Yet even the most upright are not immune to the insidious and pervasive plague of pornography sparked by pandering perverts and fanned into flames by the instant enterprise of the Internet. Read this letter written to me by a famous judge—a man who should know better than to fall for the easy traps.

"Thank you for your latest book. Over ten years ago I got rid of 'Playboy' when I started getting right with God. About a month ago, while looking for a hint to a computer game I was playing, I pulled up a hint line on the computer. The hint line was for kids, but in the middle of it, a free 'XXX' site was advertised. I was furious and decided to check it out. Outraged, I found other sites advertised in places kids would pull up. My intentions started out good, but within a month I started to sneak around after my wife left for work and tell myself I was investigating for official purposes.

"Fortunately for me, I had just started this when I read your latest book. If not for that, I probably would have kept kidding myself. You are right. I couldn't stop thinking about the images, no matter how good my intentions were. After I repented and cleansed my mind with the Word of God, I was once again at home alone and the temptation came. I recognized Satan and he fled when I confronted him with the Name of Jesus."

Morality is not always popular with society. Morality is only popular with the moral. Pornography is immoral—"soft porn" from immoral movies, and sports or fashion magazine pornography included. Morality is the quality of "rightness." Immorality is the quality of "wrong-ness." God's Word speaks in no uncertain terms to those who flirt immorally with the world, then come into His church to worship. "Ye adulterers and adulteresses, know ye not that the friendship of the world is enmity with God? whosoever therefore will be a friend of the world is the enemy of God."[2]

God gave Israel the "Mosaic Law" to keep His people forever mighty through their morality. Today the Church is God's moral agency on earth, the embassy for His moral kingdom, and Christians are His moral agents. To obey God's moral law, God gave man a moral constitution with a conscience, which fits a man with the power for both right and wrong actions. Your intellect discerns the options. Your senses appeal to one or the other. Your conscience tells you if your thoughts are right or wrong. Your will decides the issue.

Your conscience, however, can only judge based on the standard you give it. The conscience judges correctly and morally only if it has been programmed with the knowledge of God, which is the essence of morality. Conscience can be defiled or polluted, but never destroyed. Criminals act according to conscience that was programmed by people around them and the "criminal code" which they adopted. Their conscience is active, as there is even "honor among thieves," and they will act steadfast in their "loyalties." Yet their conscience does not judge correctly because they have eliminated what is truly moral by eliminating the true knowledge of God.

To the degree that you program your conscience by the Word of God, you are able to make right decisions based on "good conscience." This is why one man can commit adultery without a twinge of guilt while another cannot even read a book depicting adultery without his conscience bothering him.

In the New Testament, the new believers in the Early Church created a simple standard for their faith: "Abstain from pollution to idols, from fornication, and from things strangled and from blood."[3] Symbolically, these three translate into three standards for our faith today.

First, genuine worship of the one true God. True spirituality comes from worshiping God through the saving grace of Jesus Christ our Lord. Second, holding life sacred to God. "The life is in the blood," the Old Testament states repeatedly. Life is God's gift. The destruction or end of life is God's prerogative, not man's. To take life is immoral. Third, personal purity, which means to avoid, stay away from, and not to engage in sexual immorality.

Just a peek at an Internet porn site or a sneak sexual dalliance, a little meditation on immoral books, music or films, basically "playing footsie with the devil" seems like it could never amount to anything. But men every day are led away of their own lusts, enticed into sin. Sin brings forth death— the death of careers, reputations, relationships, freedom, unborn children.[4] *No man becomes immoral in deed without first becoming immoral in thought.*

In the sex-charged atmosphere of our modern culture, keeping ourselves pure from sexual images and immorality requires constant vigilance. The Internet pornography industry unashamedly targets 12- to 17-year-old men. It's an obvious trap, yet men—or males—fall into it every day. Ironically, one way to remain an adolescent is to do what our culture marks as "adult." *Pornography perpetuates puberty.*

Internet filters are a must, but nothing is as powerful for real help as the Word of God and the Holy Spirit.

All pornography is idolatrous. It allows you to create an image in the mind to which the act of habitual masturbation becomes an act of worship. The heart of man demands worship. God created a place in us for that purpose. The mighty Mississippi river cannot be stopped, only diverted—so also worship. God said in the Mosaic Law, "You shall not make for yourself a carved image." We cannot worship an image in our minds, or something we've posted on our walls, or looked up on our computers, and still say we worship God.

## ONE TRAP LEADS TO ANOTHER

When pornography is in the mind, a husband can easily reduce his wife to become a source for his fantasy to be fulfilled. The problem is, wives don't come airbrushed to perfection in real life. Husbands who love their wives only for sex make themselves users and predators, and her a victim or his prey. The husband no longer sees in her any value but physical, and the marriage disintegrates.

The prophet Hosea had a wife who engaged in prostitution. She loved for hire, for the gifts her lovers gave her. Her immorality was not just sexual. She also sold her emotion, her soul, for profit. It is immoral to love only for gifts. To love God only for the gifts He gives is a form of spiritual prostitution. God is to be loved because He is God! In the same way, a wife is to be loved because she is your wife. To force a wife to "love for hire," using the things you buy her as bribes, you actually reduce her to the role of a prostitute and any livelihood you provide becomes her pay.

Scripture says, "let marriage be held in honor ... and thus let the marriage bed be undefiled (kept undishonored); for

God will judge and punish the unchaste (all guilty of sexual vice) and adulterous."[5]

Men use the portion, "the marriage bed be undefiled" as license to do whatever they desire within marriage and call it "undefiled." Not so. When a man defiles his marriage bed, it is defiled. To meditate and dwell on the images of other women, and bring them into the marriage bed, is adulterous in thought. One reason pornography proliferates is that it offers intimacy, while in fact its results are actually distance and less satisfaction, often to the point of impotency. Jesus said, "Everyone who so much as looks at a woman with evil desire for her has already committed adultery with her in his heart."[6] When a wife becomes a mere body while the husband's mind goes elsewhere during times of intimacy, he merely engages in "vaginal masturbation." It's all about him, not her. The result is decreased satisfaction. Nothing she does can solve that.

The thought is parent to the deed. Any man, like the judge who secretly looked at pornography, can be led astray by his own lusts, which sow seeds of sin, and when sin is conceived, it brings death.[7] More than one kind of death exists. Financial death is bankruptcy. Marital death is divorce.

The "strange woman" whom Solomon talks about in Proverbs is anything that tantalizes a man to deceive him. The Bible describes the scene of a man led into adultery. "Suddenly he yields and follows her reluctantly like an ox moving to the slaughter, like one in fetters going to the correction to be given to a fool or like a dog enticed by food to the muzzle. Till a dart of passion pierces and inflames his vitals; then like a bird fluttering straight into the net he hastens, not knowing that it will cost him his life."[8]

The Word clearly tells a man to avoid the adulterous woman, the "strange woman," not to stray across her path nor allow his heart to desire her, because going to bed with her is the way to the chambers of death.[9]

According to news reports, both men and women now go on business trips, to high school reunions, to conventions and elsewhere, with the intention of having extramarital affairs. What the reports never give are the heartache, trauma and pain the people and their entire families experience later. We'll go into the antidote to adultery in a later chapter, but suffice it to say, *if you don't first think it, you won't later do it.*

"But remember this—the wrong desires that come into your life aren't anything new and different. Many others have faced exactly the same problems before you. And no temptation is irresistible. You can trust God to keep the temptation from becoming so strong that you can't stand up against it, for he has promised this and will do what he says. He will show you how to escape temptation's power so that you can bear up patiently against it."[10]

You don't escape *from* temptation, but *to* God. Emptying yourself of something merely leaves a hollowness which allows it to come back. Filling the space is the only remedy for lasting change. Filling our minds with the Word of God, filling our thoughts with prayer, filling our time with our wives with encouragement and appreciation—these are remedies against the negative pulls from the culture around us.

No matter what the temptation, God's covenant-keeping power is sufficient for any need. "And ye shall know the truth, and the truth shall make you free."[11]

## A Passport To Freedom

Through God's covenant with us, we can escape the bondage of sexual addictions and find the path of liberty. I started teaching the "passport to freedom" after a distraught woman introduced herself and sat down at my table in the concierge area of the Marriott Hotel in Anaheim, California.

"Are you going to talk about sex sins in your men's meeting tonight?" she asked.

"I'm not sure," I said, somewhat baffled. "Why?"

"Because my husband, who is a minister at this conference, just served me with divorce papers," she said.

Ensuing conversation made me aware he was hooked on Internet pornography. Shortly after that, at the same conference, another pastor's wife asked me to talk with her husband about his cyber-porn addiction.

Leaving that conference, I went to Newport Beach, California for a board meeting. I became curious after those ladies told me about their husbands. The next morning as I was preparing to go to the beach, read my Bible, pray and meditate, I stopped first to turn on my computer.

I typed the word "adult" into a search engine, which turned up a glut of sites featuring porn. I clicked on one of the links, and saw a picture of "hardcore" pornography. I immediately turned off the computer and spent the next few hours at the beach reading my Bible and meditating on God's Word.

Driving back to the hotel where I was staying, the picture I had seen again came to my mind. Needing to deal with it immediately, I stopped by a convenience store and bought a box of unleavened crackers and a bottle of grape juice. Back in my room, I again turned on my computer, then showered, dressed and sat down at the table.

Looking at that computer I realized it was possible to boot up my Bible program and put the Word of God in a window, then do the same with pornography, putting both windows side-by-side on one computer screen. That is exactly what happens when they are both on the one screen in your mind.

Sitting in front of the computer, I took communion with the bread and juice, and made a covenant with God in the name of Jesus Christ that nothing unclean, immoral, ungodly, perverse or lewd would ever come up on that screen again.

As a "Covenant Man," my communion was a sign of the renewing of the covenant God made with me in Christ, empowering me to keep it through the Holy Spirit.

"Ye cannot drink the cup of the Lord, and the cup of devils: ye cannot be partakers of the Lord's table, and of the table of devils."[12]

Standing up and looking down in that hotel room, I saw the table of the Lord between me and the computer which had featured the "table of devils." I would have to go past, or trample underfoot the blood and body of Christ to look at pornography on that screen again. Only a profane person would go back to that computer and pull up anything vile or sinful.

Esau traded his birthright to Jacob for a bowl of porridge, and was considered a "profane person." Worse than him, I would be selling my birthright in full knowledge of what I was doing, and would impair my relationship with the Lord. Only a fool would do such a thing.

The Bible says we *cannot*. Covenant men *cannot* partake of the table of devils. The deceitfulness of sin only shows you sin's pleasure, but never sin's consequences. There is pleasure in sin, the Bible tells us, but *the pleasure of sin only lasts for a season, while the consequences can last for a lifetime, or an eternity.*[13]

## TAKING COMMUNION

Great men of God have recognized the communion as the tool it really is. John Wesley, the evangelist, songwriter and founder of the Methodist Church took communion as much as five times each week. Smith Wigglesworth, the great healing and faith evangelist, took communion every day. They recognized that communion is a sacrament which establishes our relationship with God. It's the "Lord's table" at church or at home or on a plane, train, or in a park. It's all the Lord's table, wherever we take it. "As oft as you take it," the

Lord said, meaning we can take it as often as we need, "in remembrance of Me."

We can take communion at our wedding, on our wedding night, when we are praying for healing, or overcoming sin, as a reaffirmation of our marriage commitment, or even over our marriage bed to keep it "undefiled" and pure before God. Some couples have taken communion in front of their television set to purify themselves. Others incorporate weekly communion into their lifestyle.

A man must have moral courage to be a real man. Moral cowardice is a vice. Moral courage is a virtue.

Cowardice keeps silent. Courage speaks up for right, even if it could bring censure or criticism.

Cowardice caves in to the pressures of personalities. Courage refuses to lower standards to make them acceptable to others.

Cowardice follows doctrines of devils that tickle itching ears. Courage acts on the Proverb that says, "stop listening to doctrine that you know is wrong."[14]

Courage is necessary to manhood. I challenge you today to show yourself a man. If you are committing adultery, using your computer to look at pornography, subscribing to "porn" channels and magazines, renting "porn" movies—even if you're doing it with the full knowledge and approval of a wife or friends—I command you to repent and turn from being a profane person. Separate yourself from it, and begin to thank God for setting you free. Start with this prayer:

> "Father, I want to be a real man, without hypocrisy or feigned faith. Forgive me for my sin and lust. I want it out of my life. Out! It's undermining my faith in You, my relationship to others, and I repent. I don't just apologize, I REPENT! This is

for real. Thank you for hearing and answering my prayer. In Jesus' Name."

Now have the courage to make a communion covenant over that which is hindering you. Do it with your wife and she'll admire you!

The irresistible husband uses the tools God has given to guard his morality. When his wife knows he is true to her, in action and in thought, she can give herself unreservedly to him, knowing she can safely trust him. Free from having to perform to the level of lustful fantasies, both husband and wife can minister to each other's needs without fear. These have been ways to keep from destroying your marriage, now we can work on tools to building an indestructible marriage.

[1] John 10:10
[2] James 4:4
[3] Acts 15:2-29
[4] James 1:14-15
[5] Hebrews 13:4 AMP
[6] Matthew 5:28 AMP
[7] James 1:15
[8] Proverbs 7:22-23 AMP
[9] Proverbs 7: 25, 27
[10] I Corinthians 10:13 TLB
[11] John 8:32
[12] 1 Corinthians 10:21
[13] Hebrews 11:25
[14] Proverbs 19:27 TLB

# CHAPTER FOUR

# BE RIGHT

Getting married is easy. Staying married is the challenge. On the day of the wedding, everything looks good on the outside, but what is in the heart will always come through. And although a man can fool someone for a while, if he's missing something inside, he'll come up short in the end because *when the charm wears off, you have nothing but character left.* Many a husband has discovered this principle too late—and many a wife has, too.

## IT ALWAYS COMES DOWN TO CHARACTER

Everyone wants to be right. We all want to be the one who is proven to have the upper hand in a discussion or friendly argument. We want to know that we're right in our views and right in our actions. No one can be right all the time, but how can anyone be right at all? Good character is the only thing that makes us right—ever!

Character is the main issue in personal life, in all relationships, and in the sight of God. Character deficiency is a problem—individually, corporately, with people, companies and nations. Each generation determines its own destiny by its regard or disregard for the importance of character.

## OVERCOMING TODAY'S CHARACTER CRISIS

The world today is going through another paradigm shift philosophically and culturally. We are living in the first days that Americans have accepted lying leadership and actually applauded it. When people are willing to set aside principles for personality, they are in dangerous territory.

The most dangerous man in America is not the murderer, embezzler or slanderer, but the man who believes he is above the law. Being above the law is the epitome of lawlessness. The antichrist referred to in Scripture as coming at the end of the world is called the "lawless one." When the philosophy of a culture is such that it allows for lawless leaders, it treads on perilous ground.

During the days of the Clinton presidency, character was the determining factor in him as a person and in the nation as a whole. Self-admitted as "misleading" and engaging in an "inappropriate relationship"—euphemisms for "lying" and "adultery"—the polls still showed a high percentage of people in America had a favorable disposition toward him. Why? The "Baby Boomer" generation who voted him into office grew up with him, did as he did, thought as he thought, and therefore saw nothing that wrong with his behavior or character. Clinton's election did not reveal what the majority of Americans believed about him, but what they believed about themselves.

The "boomer" generation birthed a rebellion. As a group, if not as individuals, they are still rebels at heart. They popularized "recreational" drugs and "casual" sex. Elected to places of civil responsibility, they paraded their personal philosophies, and passed legislation allowing them to do as they pleased without regard to societal well being. Corporately, they defied the standards set forth by a previous generation, resulting in a degeneration which is continuing.

"Boomers" rebelled against "The Greatest Generation," so named in the best-selling book by Tom Brokaw. Funny thing is, that's my generation and at the time, we were just a bunch of young people like you and your friends, and we didn't think we were great. But we did have our consciences programmed according to the Word of God, which was still taught in public schools. We behaved with a moral conscience which developed our character. We did acts of heroism, patriotism, and service to humanity which the nation felt significant enough to read about in Mr. Brokaw's book.

A fringe from my generation, however, developed an existential philosophy, taught it in our universities to our children, and planted the seeds that grew into the "flower children" of the next generation. When the "boomers" grabbed hold of it, what started as an "I'm okay, you're okay" philosophy was reinterpreted, "if it feels good, do it." This degenerated to the attitude, "I want it all and I want it now." As a result, crime, debt, bankruptcy and divorce skyrocketed.

## FATHERLESSNESS CONTRIBUTES TO POOR CHARACTER

President Clinton was not just a "boomer," but also the United States' first fatherless president. Like the next generation, he had no godly father at home setting parameters and standards for life. Without such, the manhood he developed was inconsistent with the Word of God and fell outside the realm of what constitutes good character. "A good man is known by his truthfulness; a false man by deceit and lies."[1] President Theodore Roosevelt quoted George Washington as saying, "*To educate a man in mind and not in morals is to educate a menace to society.*" The lower the moral level of a society goes, the higher goes its rate of mortality.

My childhood was also basically fatherless, in that I had no fatherly role model for good behavior. My mother oversaw my upbringing and introduction to spiritual life, but my father's poor example was stronger, and for many years I determined that I would "show him," basically by "out-drinking" him. Eventually I learned that choices have consequences and my deficiency of character was hurting my future, so I chose to make a journey into God's Word to develop what I lacked.

Today's "fatherless" generation needs to make a similar decision. Men cannot expect success as a husband or father until they have built within themselves the character that is able to sustain a marriage and family. In the absence of a father's direction, finding the help we need from our eternal Father is the only way.

Cultural vices of drugs, debt and divorce feed on decayed character. Were character to be restored, most of society's problems would be solved without programs, government intervention or education. Instead, politicians today have declared it is time we "redefine America." The easiest way to destroy something is to redefine it. Communism found that method to be the perfect path to power. Hitler used the same idea in Germany with Nazism.

Redefining a nation is also the easiest way to destroy its values. In my generation, self-discipline was a virtue, but two generations later it is regarded as an anchor that holds people back from personal pleasure. A noted columnist mockingly said self-discipline is just an "antiquated sentiment designed to inhibit our ever-expanding comfort zone of inappropriate behavior."[2] The "I want it all and I want it now" mentality gives high marks to politicians regardless of character, as long as the economy is strong and we can afford to do as we please. Such politicians pander to the populace and diffuse the character issue by focusing on the "wants" and "needs" of the people. The "boomer" generation "put their own interests above the issue of character."[3]

The Bible says, "The good influence of godly citizens causes a city to prosper, but the moral decay of the wicked drives it down hill."[4]

The doctrine "boomers" have produced is:

No money—charge it!

Marital problems—divorce it!
Children's problems—let the schools fix it!
If caught—cry victim—and accuse the accusers![5]
These are not the philosophies of men with good character.

## Your Character Is An Issue Of National Importance

When asked to speak about President Harry Truman, the famed news journalist Eric Sevareid could not say he agreed with Truman's decisions, yet he conceded that to remember Truman served to "remind people what a man in that office ought to be like. It's character, just character."

The Attorney General of the State of Virginia, General Early said, "Character founded this nation; character built this nation; and character sustained this nation through wars, economic upheavals, and social injustice. No other virtue has come under such withering attack. Today we are told character doesn't matter. We are told as long as the economy is healthy and America is at peace, character is neither critical nor even relevant. This argument—which is simply a restating of the old 'ends justify the means'—has created a new dichotomy: the difference between so called public character and private character."[6]

Since the United States was founded, the Revolutionary Generation kept the infant nation alive. The Civil War Generation saved the nation. The Depression Generation kept themselves alive. The World War II Generation saved the world. The Baby Boomer Generation lived for themselves. Can the next generation save the future?

You may wonder what all this has to do with you. You may think marriage is more about money and sex than character and culture. Not so. The family is the microcosm of society. Save the family and you'll save the nation. The real question then becomes not whether your generation can save the future, but whether you as a man can first save your family.

Your stewardship of your marriage and family, and the character you develop within yourself, will determine the course of our nation more than all the politicking and sermonizing you could do in a lifetime. Sound important? It is.

You can't save a family with your grandfather's armchair religion, or your uncle's life-enhancement approach to church life. Only a heart-searching, deep hunger after God will teach you the pure character traits we used to call "sterling." Only a Holy Spirit revival can save your generation. It starts with a change of character, one person at a time.

## WHY JESUS?

The new word for today's generation is "tolerance." "Tolerance" says it doesn't make any difference what you believe, as long as you believe in God. Therefore we are told to see no difference between Muslim, Jewish, Hare Krishna, or Christianity. One is not more important than the other.

Yet if "tolerance" is correct, then the ultimate absurdity is Jesus Christ going to the Cross, when it doesn't make any difference anyway. How foolish of God to sacrifice His only Son if anyone can be saved just by thinking up a god to believe in and doing good works! The Bible says there is no other name under heaven whereby a man can be saved from hell to heaven except the Name of Jesus. No other name that can be given is acceptable to God the Father. Only Jesus!

What philosophies will we tolerate? President Clinton sincerely thought himself of good character and carried a Bible to prove it, yet held the nation in contempt by his disregard and disdain for truth in lying to the American people. Muslim men believe in character but according to the Qu'ran may have four wives legally, divorce them at their own pleasure, have as many slave girls and concubines as they wish, and rid themselves of them without thought of care or divorce. Do these philosophies matter upon which they have built their character?

Jesus is called the "cornerstone." He is all that. He is the cornerstone of your character, the bedrock upon which you can build a marriage, a family that spans generations, even an empire. Look at what Christ does for you which you cannot find elsewhere:

1. *Transformation always beats reformation.* To be reformed, and conform yourself to a code of conduct may suffice to keep you out of trouble, but being transformed by the renewing of your mind is far superior. A mind is renewed when a man meditates on God's Word to obtain His revelation and knowledge.

2. *Instruction always beats information.* We're bombarded in our "information age." But information requires no response—no action. It can be stored in memory and forgotten. God doesn't give information—He gives instruction. Instruction carries with it the necessity of, and capacity for, accomplishing of what is taught. "*The wise man is glad to be instructed, but a self-sufficient fool falls flat on his face.*"[7] "*To learn, you must want to be taught. To refuse reproof is stupid.*"[8]

3. *Wisdom is more than knowledge, but knowledge comes before wisdom.* Today's plethora of game shows and "trivia" contests prove the popularity of knowledge of any kind. Wisdom is the ability to apply knowledge for a specific, profitable purpose. God offers to give wisdom freely to any who ask for it, as often as they ask, as much as they want. No college, computer program, mentor or book can offer the same.

As I write, the "eyes of the Lord" are searching for some-one whose heart is right toward Him, to be a man He can use as a catalyst to bring change to a world in need.[9] "Despera-tion prayers" cause the sun to stand still, waters to roll back, and fire to fall from heaven as God shows Himself strong. He has promised to show Himself strong on behalf of those whose hearts are in covenant-keeping relation toward Him.

I was born eight years after the Christian milestone of the Holy Spirit outpouring at Azusa Street in Los Angeles. I grew up in the fire of the "Holiness" movement, which taught being saved, sanctified and baptized in the Holy Spirit—in that order. When I returned to Christ in my adult life, I learned to "tarry" at the altar. I spent nights walking the beach, seek-ing the Lord. I once climbed in a bathroom window of a closed church just to get to an altar to pray. That Holy Spirit outpouring was like the Colorado River—it cut deep and narrow. But today we have developed a "seeker sensitive" church which is more like the Mississippi at flood tide—cov-ering a lot of territory, but not as deep in many ways.

The church I grew up in wasn't concerned about making the unsaved comfortable, but making God pleased. The evi-dence of God's pleasure were signs, wonders, miracles and gifts of the Holy Spirit. Both the gifts and fruit of the Spirit had to be balanced in the life. Supernaturally sustained, the church hungered after God in a flesh-denying, Spirit-control-ling, Christ-centered way that brought glory to God and man. As the years passed, the balance and message became diluted and enmeshed in the world, or legalistic and no longer rel-evant to the culture.

*It has always been God's way to meet a contemporary generation with a contemporary ministry.* To build deep char-acter once again, you need your revelation from God just as the previous generation needed theirs. "Life Enhancement Christians" go to church to try to meet temporal needs, which is disappointing at best and nauseating at worst. You don't need a "drive by" religion on Sunday morning. You need a 24-hour-a-day lifestyle in Christ.

"Where there is no revelation, the people cast off restraint; but happy is he who keeps the law."[10] Your generation needs a contemporary ministry that isn't a watered-down version of a dead movement, but a fresh revelation of the power of God for a generation in desperate need of a Savior.

"You shall not take the name of the Lord in vain,"[11] God commanded His people. God's Name and his character are inseparable. To profane His Name is to defame His character. How can a man use His Name in profanity, then worship that same Name in church? All profanity is based on taking God's Name in vain.

Equally profane is to call yourself by His Name, "Christian," without His personal approval to use it. Only Christ has the right to approve your use of His Name. You receive that permission when you are born again. Calling yourself a Christian when you have no intention of living like one is vanity.

## YOU ARE WHAT YOU THINK

What creates our character? For at least the last two presidential elections, political pundits and nervous nominees have wondered aloud and talked about whether character even matters. Many say all that matters is how a person acts, and not what he thinks, which begs the question, can a man have good character and bad thoughts? Or is there even a difference between a man's thought life and his character? The answer is simple: No!

"As a man thinketh, so is he,"[12] the Bible says. What a man thinks and believes determines what he is. Character stems from thoughts. Thoughts are filtered by philosophies or creeds—philosophies we ingest from the world around us.

Many a man has felt guilty for a stray or random thought over which he felt no control, which simply flitted through his mind. These are often not our own thoughts, but elements from the world around us, or even satanic temptations that are not ours to own. Only when we take such thoughts into our hearts to meditate on them, making them "high places" in our minds to which we run for escape or comfort, are they sin to us. *Out of your heart springs the issues of life, so it is your heart you must protect.*

Character cannot make its own standards. It has no self-creative nor corrective powers. The best character is still in constant need of checks and balances—stimulus from without—lest it run to excesses or fail in development. Character deteriorates as everything in life deteriorates, unless it is fed from external sources. The purity of the external sources on which it feeds determines the strength of the character. Which means, thoughts pondered in the heart make or break a man.

What a man thought was of utmost importance to Jesus. He asked His disciples, "Whom do men say that I am?" They answered that people thought He was John the Baptist, or Elijah, or Jeremiah, or one of the prophets.[13] Interesting that everyone was wrong! Then Jesus asked, "Who do you say that I am?" Our answer to His question is the greatest determination of our character. When we get it right, we're right.

## Going For Greatness

*Talent can take a man to a place that his character cannot sustain.* Some of the greatest athletes in the world have suffered because their talent took them to a level which their character was too frail to uphold. Many men become famous, but few become truly great. Fame can come in a moment, but greatness comes with longevity.

Two real men I won't name—one in football, the other in baseball—both hit the top at about the same time, and both fell into eclipse. The football player returned to his faith and meditated on God's Word, which developed a character that could support his tremendous ability. He returned to his sport, became a great player, and took his team all the way to a Super Bowl. The baseball player continued to depend on his talent without trying to rebuild his character, and has suffered the anguish and shame of his lifestyle off the playing field, and his inability to get back on it.

You can have talent, but it's your character that will win you the promotion, build the career, launch you into greater enterprises, and keep you married.

The typical man tries to mature without investing in his own character. Until the last twenty years there were literally no classes or teaching about manhood. Still today, only from a relatively few places can a man can find material challenging enough to produce real change.

God has given these character-building tools to every man:

*Knowledge* - Knowledge is the acquiring of facts, the possession of truth. No greater resource for knowledge is known to man than God's Word.

*Understanding* - Understanding is the interpretation of those facts. Meditating on the Word and praying for revelation gives clarity and understanding.

*Wisdom* - Wisdom is the application of knowledge. "If any man lacks wisdom let him ask of God Who gives liberally."[14] Wisdom is acquired after knowledge and understanding, simply by asking.

*Authority* - Authority in public life stems from righteousness in private life. Just as decisions translate into energy, righteousness translates into authority.

*Confidence* - Confidence comes as the result of trusting what has been planted within the inner man. Confidence in Christ within you is far superior to self-confidence.

*Maturity* - Maturity starts with the acceptance of responsibility. Some men are mature at 17 while others are still immature at 70. Accepting responsibility for self is a necessary step to accepting responsibility for a wife or an entire family.

The knowledge of truth comes first. "Where there is ignorance of God, crime runs wild; but what a wonderful thing it is for a nation to know and keep His laws."[15] Only one moral, ethical, and true foundation to right character exists, and that is truth. Truth is good character's unassailable and indestructible basis. Opinions do not hold up to truth. Truth must be sought after, studied out, learned and rehearsed to develop good character.

What do you think about God, man, duty and truth? What have you pulled into your inner man and adopted as your beliefs? Jesus said, "I am the Way, the Truth and the Life."[16] To know Jesus is to open the door to Truth.

First in life you learned to listen, then to speak, after that came reading and last writing. For this reason, newspapers are called the "fourth estate." Listening, not speaking, is the basic art of communication. You started learning to listen even in the womb. Odd how some men regress instead of progress in listening ability. The world's poorest salesman always talks past the point of the sale. *You don't make a success in life by your ability to speak, but by your ability to listen.*

One of the most common complaints of all wives is; "My husband hears me, but he doesn't listen to me." Talking to your wife instead of listening to her is like building your life on talent and personality instead of principle and character. It will only take you so far, then you'll collapse.

Your best friend and worst enemy are both with you right now. They're not Jesus or the devil. They're you. Right where you are, you have the potential to become one of thousands of disappointments, or one of God's few successes, based on your love for truth. "A wise man loves instruction, but a self-confident fool falls flat on his face."[17] In other words, it's hard to tell somebody something they think they already know. Is that you? What kind of a man are you?

## WHERE ARE YOU ON THE CHARACTER SCALE?

The Bible exhorts you and I to live righteously. "Let us draw near with a true heart in full assurance of faith, having our hearts sprinkled from an evil conscience, and our bodies washed with pure water. Let us hold fast the profession of our faith without wavering; (for he is faithful that promised;) And let us consider one another to provoke unto love and to good works: Not forsaking the assembling of ourselves together, as the manner of some is; but exhorting one another: and so much the more, as ye see the day approaching."[18]

A man will generally learn something about character from his father, for better or worse, and then from associating with others. This is why the Apostle Paul stated clearly, "Do not be misled: Bad company corrupts good character."[19] It's a sad commentary on us as men that when we hear of a man going out with "the guys," the first thing we think of is sin.

*A man's character is known by his friends*, the Proverb says, not by his bank account. Friends are life's greatest treasure or life's greatest trial. You cannot choose a father, mother, sister or brother—but you can choose your friends. The friends you choose can be a blessing or a cursing. They can help you build good character, or help lead you down an unsavory path of poor choices.

I introduced my grown grandson at a meeting and asked him to say a word to the throng of young men and women who were attending. He stood casually and quoted the Apostle

Paul, then said, "It was when I changed my friends that I was able to change my life. I knew as long as I continued to hang out with them I would just keep hanging. So I made the choice."

Making right choices helps you build good character.

The "Irresistible Husband" is a man of good character, a trustworthy man, a man of his word, one with moral worth and value—not an angel, just a "guy" who wants to do right and really be a man. When this man of character sins, he is willing to repent, to God and to his wife. He is not afraid to accept responsibility for his failures.

The "Irresistible Husband" understands the value of good relationships and the need for communication. He knows that by aiming at the smallest microcosm in society, his family and indeed his own character, he can reshape his world. He understands that, "It is wiser to rule your spirit than take a city."[20]

1   Proverbs 12:17 TLB
2   "Boomers by Design Fail Leadership Test," by Paul G. Labadie, USA Today, October 14, 1998, page 15A.
3   Mr. Robert Jordan, "The Boston Globe," July 12, 1998.
4   Proverbs 11:11 AMP
5   Ibid, Jordan
6   Copied in personal letter from Commonwealth of Virginia, January 21, 1999, David E. Johnson, Counsel to the Attorney General.
7   Proverbs 10:8 TLB
8   Proverbs 14:1
9   Proverbs 18:16
10  Proverbs 29:18 NKJV
11  Exodus 20:7
12  Proverbs 23:7
13  Mark 8:27-29
14  James 1:5
15  Proverbs 29:18 TLB
16  John 14:6
17  Proverbs 10:8 TLB
18  Hebrews 10:22-25
19  1 Corinthians 15:33 NIV
20  Proverbs 16:32

# CHAPTER FIVE

# WAKE UP

Two hunters were walking through the woods. Suddenly one turned to the other and said, "Hey, today's Sunday."

The other replied, "Oh, that's okay, I couldn't have gone to church anyway. My daughter is sick."

Why wake up and go to church when there are so many other things to do on Sunday? Why not watch a Christian message on television, sing along to Christian music on the radio, and just send a check for your tithes or offerings?

Church is God's sanctuary, the doorway to heaven where His people gather together with one mind and one purpose, to worship Him. Church is the common ground of your family, where territories no longer exist, and husband and wife, father and children meet on neutral turf to listen together to the wisdom of the Word. It is the source of new areas of mutual interest and new topics for conversation that last all week long.

Regardless of who was mad at whom, how hurt or disappointed you may have been the previous week, or what successes or joys you may have achieved, knowing you have that steady appointment for church is a form of accountability that has helped to balance generations. With children, no matter who went to which birthday party or game, or where anyone shopped or ate, come Sunday mornings, family members have a "date" with God that when kept, promotes consistency, discipline, and unity within the family.

The church is also the institution that establishes a Christian culture based on God's moral law. *The Church is your bulwark against the culture of the world.*

Your presence in church contributes to its power in the community. Failure to be a part of a church diminishes the ability of the Church as a whole to contribute to society.

I read a newspaper article in one city about a debate among civic leaders who wanted to tax churches so they would have to pay "their share" for the provision of the city's services. They said the church's non-profit status was a benefit taken at the expense of other citizens. These civic leaders showed no understanding whatsoever as to what Christian churches accomplish for society.

For example, the ministry of just one church prayed and counseled a young couple who had decided to divorce. As a result they were reunited. Since she had helped him launch his career at the expense of her own, if they had divorced, she would have had to file for welfare, receive tax breaks for aid to dependent children, and use public health services at a total cost of approximately $50,000 per year to the government. Since they didn't divorce, he continued in his career, which increased his tax base, so they paid more taxes while at the same time being involved in schools and other community activities.

This one church and its ministry to one couple saved the city, county, state and federal governments thousands of dollars in just one instance, without costing taxpayers a cent. In person after person and church after church and community after community, such stories play out every day.

Due to the prison ministry of one church, an inmate was converted to Christ, which reduced the rate of recidivism in the penal institution and saved the tax rolls nearly $50,000 per year. In one church, one drug addict came to Christ, stopped stealing, stopped defacing public property, no longer needed rehabilitation, and went to work. That saved the community another $35,000, saved homeowners far more because of what he would have stolen from them, and increased the tax rolls as he became a solid citizen.

One usher in one church had been an alcoholic and became a staunch believer. His health improved, saving insurance expenses, hospital requirements, and eventual nursing home space. His rate of absenteeism dropped at work, saving his company money, increasing their profits which increased their tax. His children stopped using drugs and no longer needed public health centers for counseling. His wife stopped worrying and put her energies into her career and into the local battered women's shelter. In total, this was roughly a savings of $100,000 from that one family, plus increased benefits to the community from every family member for years to come.

Just one church I visited last Sunday, with 4,000 in membership, may have saved the local, state and federal governments millions of dollars in services.

The Church is the strongest voice we have against false beliefs such as cults that cause people to harm others. It is a patriotic place that encourages volunteerism to local causes and faithfulness to the national interest. Its members vote to support honest leadership. They give far more per capita to charitable causes than unchurched citizens. Its missionaries sent out with the gospel message contribute to world peace. Its evangelists bring in the poor, homeless, and destitute, giving them fresh opportunities in life. Its teachers inspire leaders, athletes and successful career people to be better, share more, contribute to the good of all.

Does the local movie theater do that? The corner barroom? The City Planning Commission? The hospital? The police force? Jesus Christ's Church does what no other institution on earth does!

## What Is Church To Me?

Eleven apostles and 3,000 people attended the birthing of Jesus' Church. The apostles were chosen by Jesus, not by a church. He chose *them*—they did not choose *Him*. They received their authority directly from the Lord, not from the Church. They were not designated by the Church, but before the Church was ever born, they were anointed, appointed, given authority, commissioned to make disciples, and sent to preach the Gospel. The Lord gave them commandments and directions as He discipled them. Our Lord won them, trained them and sent them.

Their ministry was not a development of or from a church, but the Church came from them. This is the Lord's pattern for His Church today. First the ministry—then the Church. Ministry determines what the Church is, not vice versa. The Church serves as the womb from which ministries are birthed. The ministries that are birthed then define what the Church becomes to the culture around it.

Are you attending church? Are you in ministry there? The most enjoyable ministry you'll know as your family is young is one you can share with your wife and children.

My niece and her husband engaged in nursing home ministry when their children were small. The nursing home residents imbibed the vigor and energy of the children that crawled over and under their wheelchairs and asked dozens of silly questions. The family drew values from their efforts as mother and father taught the children about respect for elders, aging, living, and dying.

Friends from California took as their family ministry feeding the hungry in the barrio district near their church. As their sons went through their teens, two Sundays each month were set aside for the family to minister together and no member missed it. During those years, the family witnessed one of the worst drug-infested neighborhoods in Southern California transform into a law-abiding community and a new church planted after many years of labor. Books cannot teach what you, your wife and family can learn by ministering together.

Ministers and ministries are "called out" to bring people into right relationship with God through Jesus Christ. All who are born again become members of the Church as a whole. As the Church grows, the ministry grows. The Church needs your ministry. Your ministry needs the Church.

## THE SABBATH IS HOLY

"Remember the Sabbath day, to keep it holy," God said to Israel through Moses. That doesn't just mean church attendance.

Recent studies are proving what many of us feel, that most people today are sleep deprived. We have more timesaving inventions and appliances than any time in history, yet we still can't find time to rest. We buy the fastest modems, subscribe to the fastest Internet connections, yet still don't have time to get everything done that we're trying to do. Caught up in the pressures of living, we think if we do more, we'll accomplish or have more, so we become slaves to our lifestyles.

The Sabbath stands for a day of rest. It's a day of setting aside work to worship. *The Sabbath is a day of rejoicing because our ability to rest proclaims that we are not slaves but free men.*

The Sabbath in the Old Testament became the Lord's day in the New. There are no "first day of the week" laws in the New Testament because it is a day of love, not law. Jesus taught that we were not created for the Sabbath, but the Sabbath was created for us.

Christ arose on the first day of the week, so the Early

Church met that day, and we have continued since.[1] Jesus appeared to His disciples on the first day of the week.[2] The disciples were commissioned to preach on the first day of the week.[3] The Holy Spirit was imparted on the first day of the week.[4] The Day of Pentecost was on the first day of the week.[5] The Book of Revelation was given to the Apostle John on the first day of the week.[6] The early Christians took offerings on the first day of the week.[7]

Unlike some calendars today, Sunday is not the end of the week, but the first day of the week. In the Old Testament, God's people lived based on sight, sense and circumstance. Looking back on the previous week, they gave their tithes and thanked God for what already was. In the New Testament, we operate based on faith, spirit and Word. We look forward to the coming week, and give God the first day of it.

The Sabbath created by the Old Covenant mirrored God resting on the seventh day at the end of the week. In the New covenant, we celebrate the finished work of salvation and new creation in Christ Jesus as a way to start a new week. And we rest.

Lack of rest creates tension, friction, irritability, touchiness, and a host of maladies. When those give birth to strife, then the Bible says "every evil thing" follows.[8] Resting is crucial to relationships.

Whatever day we declare as our Sabbath, we say, "Lord, how can I honor You on this day? I want this to be Your day, Lord, not mine." It is a holy day unto the Lord. By keeping it holy, God promises He will add hours to our days.[9]

## JESUS' TWO CHURCH MEMBERSHIPS

Jesus' earthly parents raised Him in the church His Father established. They trained Him in the scriptures and took Him to the temple. Throughout His life He was often found in synagogues. The priests of His day loved ostentatious displays of "holiness" and were slaves to tradition, emphasizing externals while playing a role for profit. Out of respect for His Father's church, Jesus paid His temple tax in spite of the local leadership. Jesus spoke words of life to men dying of meaningless rituals. He did not refrain from giving health and life on the Sabbath or in the synagogue.

Out of the Jewish faith, Jesus drew twelve men to Himself and taught them the truths of the new covenant, as based on the old. Into the spiritually moribund and carnally-led church, He brought new light, life and truth. His new Church started within the old. Not all believed in Him or His message, but those who did found life more abundantly.[10]

Jesus continued to love the church of His Father until the time of His crucifixion. He submitted to the arrest and trial by church leaders, although they were themselves despicable. He was killed by the very church He loved. Yet His death became the means of new life for the Church. His disciples continued in the Jewish church until its leaders, opposing their miracles and doctrines, ostracized and persecuted them. The disciples gave their lives for truth, and from their sacrifices came what we know as the "Christian" Church. It is a Church called by His Name, and one in which He still gives life through the indwelling of His Spirit because of the resurrection.

It is easy for any institution to harden to the principles upon which it was established. This is true not just in some denominations and churches, but also in almost every institution of higher education in the world today.

Our choice determines if the sacrifices made for a new, better Church will be of effect, or if we will allow our churches to become the spiritual wastelands that Jesus came to resurrect. We can be in our church what Jesus wanted to be in His Church. We can complete His mission, fulfill His desires, answer His prayers, by doing and being in our church all that He would do and be.

Why wake up on Sundays? Because an irresistible husband is faithful to the house of worship. He loves the Lord's Church. He doesn't have to be bribed, dragged, or coaxed to attend church with his wife or family, but instead leads his family in attendance, teaching them the importance and value God places on His Son's Church, and recognizing the price it cost Him to start it.

1 Mark 16:9; Acts 20:7
2 Mark 16:11; John 20:19
3 John 20:21
4 John 20:22
5 Acts 2:1
6 Revelation 1:10
7 I Corinthians 16:2
8 James 3:16
9 Proverbs 10:27
10 John 10:10

# CHAPTER SIX

# STOP THE CURSE!

"I'll never forgive my father for what he did to me."

"My mother never acted like a real mother to me."

"When my parents divorced, I never really saw my father again."

"I hate my mother because of the men she married and brought into our home."

We've all heard such statements, and perhaps even said similar things ourselves. It seems as though when we marry, we should be able to start a life on our own and forget about everything that happened in our past. Yet we have learned from sitcoms and counseling sessions and B-rated movies and high school psychology courses that the way we were raised and the feelings we have toward our parents can haunt us throughout life, at least in our relationships.

God's Word says two people become "one flesh" in marriage, yet how often does it seem like six people are crowding in, maybe more? Each spouse's parents, stepparents, custodial grandparents, all vie for a spot in the marriage relationship. Many good books exist that tackle such issues, so I'll go straight to the point and deal with the spiritual remedy and its benefits. If you'll take the remedy, you'll be able to bask in its blessings.

## RELEASE

Parents are imperfect at best and psychotically cruel at worst. Jesus taught us by example how to deal with both imperfections and cruelties. No one was ever more cruel to another living person than Jesus' so-called friends, the government, and His Church were to Him. His physical torture may have been surpassed, but Christ's mental, emotional and spiritual anguish has no match because He had no match—He was perfect, and therefore blameless before God and man, completely undeserving of anything He suffered. Yet in return for the indignities and brutalities He suffered at their hands, Jesus said, "Father, forgive them."[1] With those words, He opened a door whereby we can each be forgiven and follow Him from death into eternal life in Heaven.

After Jesus' resurrection, He appeared to His disciples and "breathed on them," then He said, "Receive the Holy Ghost. Whose sins you retain they are retained and whose sins you remit they are remitted."[2] The pattern is the same today for us to become free from all that others have done to us and against us. We receive by faith the Holy Spirit, then we forgive.

The Bible says that if we have "ought," which means a grudge or unforgiveness, against another, we are to leave our gift on the altar—meaning our worship, our giving, our ministry, our talent—and go to the person to make it right. Yet many of us live for years mad at parents, and feeling justified about it. Such unforgiveness and bitterness hurts us and can irreparably damage our marriages. We must forgive.

How do you forgive someone who beat you up? Someone who sexually molested you? Someone who violated your trust? How do you forgive the one who kicked you out of the house when you were too young to leave? The truth is, you can't forgive them with unconditional love no matter how hard you try. To forgive, you need God's Spirit. You need His unconditional forgiveness, without blame or judgment, which becomes a free gift to the person that they do not deserve. Only Jesus can give it to you, and empower you to give it to them. There is no other way.

*Forgiveness is God's greatest gift.* If Jesus lived His entire life, died and was resurrected, but had never forgiven us, heaven would still be closed to us. When He forgave, he allowed us to be free from sin, which qualifies us to enter heaven one day. When we forgive sins, we release them out of our lives, and release the other person to be forgiven as well. When we forgive sins, we open heaven to the other person, no matter how much they don't deserve it. Jesus didn't deserve what He got, and the people He forgave didn't deserve His forgiveness. Yet He took that unjust punishment and forgave. No matter what unjustified events have occurred in your life—from an angry parent or a girlfriend who dumped you—you can become free from their sin, and release them as well, by your forgiveness.

We cannot bear the sins of others. Only Jesus could do that. Forgiveness is God's way to set us free from others' sins. Unforgiveness closes. Forgiveness opens. Unforgiveness binds. Forgiveness releases. Unforgiveness constitutes hardness of heart. Forgiveness constitutes liberality, generosity, and freedom.

## REAL MEN DON'T WITHHOLD FORGIVENESS

The refusal to forgive may be the most heinous sin of all. Listen to what God says. "For if ye forgive men their trespasses, your heavenly Father will also forgive you: But if ye forgive not men their trespasses, neither will your Father forgive your trespasses."[3] There is no way around forgiveness. It is a hurdle a man must leap to prove himself a real man. He must help his wife and children to forgive others as well—maybe even to forgive him.

Learning forgiveness, then practicing forgiveness creates a way of life, a habit which often doesn't require conscious thought. We see that quality occasionally in people, and their generous spirit draws others to them.

Forgiveness is not a one-time deal. Jesus told Peter we are to forgive "seventy times seven,"[4] which is to say, continually. There will never be a time on this earth when forgiveness is unnecessary or passe.

I have a friend named James whose father is a major part of his and his children's lives. They get along great now, but it wasn't always so. James, when I first met him, was embittered and angry with his dad. A twenty-year alcoholic and rage-aholic, his father had made James' life a living hell growing up. James was angry, felt betrayed, ashamed, mistrustful. He wanted to love his dad, but could not understand how his dad could have been so cruel to James as a child.

At first James had no thought about the terrible weight of guilt his father was experiencing, the fear and shame that covered him. Godly counsel, prayer, and the reality of God's Word gripped James' heart and he forgave his father out of obedience to God's command. When he did, he felt as though he was being crucified for a sin he hadn't committed. But he remembered Jesus' total innocence and he prayed as Jesus prayed, "Father forgive him."

Once we've forgiven, we are qualified to ask for others to forgive us. James' father made his own decisions. But because he fell in a big way didn't make James innocent by comparison. James needed his father to forgive James his sins, especially his bitterness, just as James needed to forgive the father. When James went to his father to ask for forgiveness, the years of anger, mistrust and shame began to fade away. James' gift of forgiveness made all the difference in his father, and over the years they have built the strong relationship they had missed.

Forgiving others requires prayer and consideration. The person you need to forgive may not be available, or open to hear you forgive them. You can create even more trouble for yourself by telling someone you forgive them when they don't believe they need forgiveness. Yet if you've forgiven them in private, you are qualified to ask openly for their forgiveness.

No matter how rocky it may seem or how hard at first, the man who carries God's forgiveness in his heart is irresistible to others. My friend John Karr says, "The devil is resistible, God is irresistible." So true.

God does not give invitations, He gives commands. "Forgive," He says, as a command to you today. He also commanded, "Honor your father and mother." Forgiving them is the first step.

## HONORING PARENTS MAKES YOU LIVE WELL

The Apostle Paul rephrased God's commandment slightly, "Honor thy father and mother; (which is the first commandment with promise;) That it may be well with thee, and thou mayest live long on the earth."[5]

The benefits Paul interpreted from the Law were that if we honored our parents we would "live well." God established parents as authority figures. We receive our first impression about God from our parents. Honoring elders pays a debt to the past. If a parent has done nothing else deserving honor, at least we honor them for giving us life.

I have a successful friend named John Binkley, whom I've written about at various times. No matter what John accomplishes, God seems to give him even more success. No matter what John earns, he seems to receive even more through many side benefits that are unmistakably God's blessings.

All of John's blessings started when he was struggling, trying to make it from paycheck to paycheck, yet he became obedient to God's Word. John and his wife Sharon noticed one small part of the Bible that said we are to take care of our parents even before we take care of the church.[6] They jointly decided they would start supplementing their parents' incomes, even though John and Sharon still had teenaged boys at home and barely enough for their own needs. They also tithed and gave to their local church as generously as they could at the time. Since then, John has increased in his ability and efforts to be a giver, and has never looked back. As John and Sharon have testified about how God honored them for honoring their parents, others have copied them.

I was working on this book when a friend named George called me to invite me to dinner at a fancy steakhouse he liked. George is very reserved, quiet, and even though I've known him for a number of years, I've never known his background. Over dinner, I started asking questions. He said that since he'd heard about John Binkley helping his parents, he'd had some personal breakthroughs as well. Then he told me a story that absolutely astonished me.

Sitting in that well-appointed dining room, with George looking every bit the business success he has become, no one would have guessed his background. He told me he was raised by a mother who had had several husbands. She lived with her many children in the projects of their city. By the time George was a young teenager, his family had been kicked out of every public assistance housing project in their city for non-payment of rent. Finally, George realized he had no future by staying home with his mother and siblings, so he struck out on his own to find his biological father. His father was moderately successful, and agreed to take George in, taught him his trade, and decided the decent thing to do was take George to a church, even though he didn't go himself. George committed his life to Christ and eventually married a beautiful woman who helped him rise to the top of his profession.

With the children grown, and being well established in his church, George's life had pretty much plateaued. No one knew of his past and he never saw the need to share it. Then he heard John Binkley's testimony about caring for parents.

George was conscience-stricken, realizing that although he'd done all he could for his mother, she was still living the life of an indigent, was often unkempt, and had never been open to the Gospel. George and his wife decided that instead of buying her a house or a car or something with strings attached, as they always had, they would simply write her a check and send it to her. They did. Month after month they wrote checks and sent them to George's mom, with no expectation of thanks, nor any questions as to how she spent the money. Then the breakthrough came.

As George and his wife were sitting in church one Sunday morning, a woman entered the back door and shuffled down the side aisle all the way to the front of the church. Even from the corner of his eye, George recognized the limp gait and ill-fitting clothing and realized his mother was at church. She walked up to the preacher who was well into his Sunday message and stopped him to ask, "Do you know where my son George is?" George raised his hand to the pastor and she waved at him, then took a seat on the front row. George overcame his embarrassment and rejoiced that his mother had finally shown an interest in his God. Week after week George's mother has now come to church and sat on the front row, without a commitment yet, but with a new look in her eye that George has never before seen, like she's finally seeing "the light."

What happened? George stopped trying to make his mother fit some image, or rehabilitate her, or do what he considered to be in her best interests, and he simply honored her by giving to her. He put his money where his mouth was and said, "I love you," in a way that touched his mother's heart more than anything he'd ever said or done.

John's return for honoring his parents is tangible. George's return is intangible, and something money could never buy. The way you honor your parents may vary, and the way you'll see a return on the promise will also vary, for the promise is simply "well being," meaning whatever will make you well.

## The Next Generation

Men who forgive and honor their parents don't simply make things better for their parents or for themselves, they blaze the trail on which their children will walk. Recently my daughter took a trip with her son, driving halfway across the nation together. They were discussing how his grandfather, her father-in-law, had been an alcoholic but had now been sober for thirty years. Even more remarkable, his alcoholism had not surfaced in the next generation. My daughter's husband, through forgiving his father, had released that sin out of his life, and out of his house. His children are now walking after his footsteps, not after the previous generation.

"Generational sins" or "curses" transfer from one age to the next by men and women who refuse to deal with them when they have the opportunity. Filled with anger and unforgiveness, although they may not copy the same sins, they keep the spirit of that sin alive in their family and it is transferred to their children instead of stopped cold.

Regardless of what your parents did or didn't do to you, you can forgive them today and stop the curse. There's no need for you to live with the effects of their sin, nor for you to pass it along to your own children.

Once you've forgiven your parents, you can honor them, which may take many forms. If you don't even know your parents, you can still honor them by thanking God that they were His tools to give you life. And you can honor your spiritual parents as well, caring for them, writing to them, appreciating them. In this way you become honorable in God's eyes and begin to live as a man of honor.

[1]  Luke 23:34
[2]  John 20:22-23
[3]  Matthew 6:14-15
[4]  Matthew 18:22
[5]  Exodus 20:12; Ephesians 6:2-3
[6]  I Timothy 5:4

# CHAPTER SEVEN

# SET YOUR JUDGMENT

"The worlds are framed (upheld) by the word of His power."[1] God's Word upholds the entire universe, the creation of it, the maintenance and sustenance of it. Because you are created in God's image, as God's Word is to Him, so your word is to you. Therefore, your world is framed by your words, which are your power.

When you walk in forgiveness, words of anger, bitterness, acrimony, rancor, and rage are no longer part of your life, so they do not become faulty building blocks on which you frame a teetering home. Yet other words can create just as shaky a foundation for your home, words for which we are told by God that we will have to give an account.[2] This means, when we're jealous of someone's new boat, disappointed at being turned down for a raise, frustrated with wife or children, what comes out of our mouths will condemn us or commend us.

Our words determine how we are judged. They set our judgment. When we complain that our wife is self-absorbed, we set a judgment for ourselves the next time we become preoccupied with our own interests. When we yell at a child for spilling the milk, we set the judgment whereby the rest of the family will judge us the next time we spill the milk. We give an account on earth and in heaven for every word we speak.

Words have creative power. A man who controls his tongue is a man of power. He can speak blessing, honor, promotion, peace and life. Into his family he can speak health, good grades, a willing attitude and love.

Early in my marriage, my wife suffered a heart-wrenching miscarriage, which threw her into compounded pain, mental anguish, and uncontrollable bleeding. Frightened and unaware of what to do, suddenly it struck me that before we rushed to the doctor, I could pray over her and speak words of life and healing over that situation. We prayed in agreement and immediately the bleeding stopped. In a short time the pain subsided, and with it peace returned to her mind.

A doctor friend whom I greatly admire had an ailing baby for whom his doctor friends did all they could. When Dino walked into the hospital room late one night and looked at little Katie through the maze of tubes and wires, he saw she was turning blue, and as he stretched out his hand, her little foot was completely cold. Suddenly faith rose up within Dino and he spoke to his daughter, "I choose life. Live!" Life sprang into the child's body, and she is well today, thriving under the care of her faith-filled parents.

That is how powerful your words are. *You literally shape the world around you, and set your own judgment with your own words.*

## Murder vs. Grace

Jesus spoke ninety-four words about the Sabbath. He spoke only four words about killing. Murder, however, is about more than physical killing. Murder contains factors of unlawfulness, premeditation, and maliciousness. Murder is the deliberate taking of a life which was created in the image of God. Murder is sacrilegious in its violence and injustice. When God said, "thou shalt not kill," he showed the value He gave life, which He created for His family.

Murder begins and proceeds from the heart, and is developed in thoughts and meditations of the mind. In the new covenant, Jesus elevated and expanded the act of murder to give it a spiritual dimension. He said, "Whoever harbors anger and hatred against a brother has committed murder already in his heart and is in danger of God's judgment."[3]

People can murder other people's dreams, ideas, reputation and faith. A father can murder his child's aspirations. A husband can murder his wife's self image. A son can murder his mother's good intentions. Murder is a damnable act, whether in heart, mind or body. As humans, we are no different from those perverse beings who preferred a murderer to be set free and Jesus Christ, the Son of God, crucified. Every time we choose words to express murderous feelings in our hearts, we choose murder over Jesus Christ.

There is a solution to murderous words and the emotions of murder in our hearts. Grace. As LaFayette Scales teaches, "We have nothing to give anyone other than the grace of God that is in Christ Jesus our Lord."

Grace gives mercy, eliminates judgment, provides forgiveness, erases anger and expresses the nature of ministry. Grace manifests reconciliation, understanding, and love which is found in no other place in no other way. Grace accepts duty and obligation, but allows liberty and freedom. Grace is divine, what it offers is human.

Jesus Christ brought grace and truth into a world deplorably void of either. He showed us that truth is the foundation for the way we live and the life we have, and that grace is our only means to attain it. Whether saving our souls from sin, or the salvation of relationships dear and precious to us, grace is the key.

*God's grace is amazing because we live in a world almost totally without it.* Tragedies in human lives today reveal the sad lack of grace. Genocide taking place on a global scale, rampant slavery, pimping, racism, cultural and tribal "cleansing," raging hatred that stirs groups to violence and war, STD's ruining children and adults alike, and divorce decimating families everywhere—all are the result of a dearth of grace.

God's grace can take a man living in the lowest "gutter-most" and raise him to live in the highest uttermost. It takes grace!

A crusty slave trader in a jail cell knew the liberty the grace of God gave him, and in gratitude penned the song, "Amazing Grace." It is still one of the best-known and best-loved songs in the world, sung by all, because of the quickening power of the Holy Spirit when it was written. The anointing abides!

Scripture tells us the Early Church had "great grace."[4] They showed their grace by giving their earthly possessions and sharing with others. *You can give without loving, but you cannot love without giving.* Grace developed their art of giving.

The Pharisees had little grace—or none—and the church at Corinth had "cheap grace." The Corinthians allowed known sinners into membership in good standing. Incest was allowed to have a place in the heart and life of a couple in the congregation. During communion, church members ate and drank to excess, not discerning the Lord's body when they ate the bread and drank the wine, and as a result many were sick and some died.[5] It is a dreadful thing to fall into the hands of an angry God. Horrifying to be without grace.

Philip Yancey in his book, *What's so Amazing About Grace* tells of "grace abuse." A minister friend told him he was divorcing his wife and marrying a younger woman because she made him feel good. Philip asked him, "What about your wife? What about God? What about your ministry?"

His friend replied, "I'm leaving the ministry and when I get ready, I'll come back."

He willfully abused the grace of God. Years later when Philip saw him again, he was working at a secular company, and had no thought of God or ministry. He desecrated God's gift, defiled his wife, and would suffer the consequences for an eternity. He abused the grace God gave him.

The man preferred obeying his feelings to obeying God's Word. What effrontery! Not only did he profane the sacred gifts and grace of God, but by his actions, he called God a liar. "He who does not believe God [in this way] has made Him out to be and represented Him as a liar."[6]

Rahab is listed in the lineage of Jesus. Though classed as a harlot, the grace in her heart caused her to hide God's servants, sparing their lives. God's grace then spared her family when her city was demolished.

Zaccheus, a short man, publican and tax collector heard Jesus was passing by, and climbed up in a tree to see him. Jesus called Zaccheus down saying He wanted to dine at his house. Zaccheus' response showed the grace that came with the invitation. "Zacchaeus stood before the Lord and said, 'Sir, from now on I will give half my wealth to the poor, and if I find I have overcharged anyone on his taxes, I will penalize myself by giving him back four times as much!' Jesus told him, 'This shows that salvation has come to this home today. This man was one of the lost sons of Abraham, and I, the Messiah, have come to search for and to save such souls as his.'"[7]

Restitution is an element of faith that followed Zaccheus' repentance. Restitution means making right, or giving back, what was wrongfully done or wrongfully taken. Whether a pack of cigarettes as a boy at a convenience store, or the taking of a girl's virginity as a teenager, Jesus said to Zaccheus that restitution and repentance was the evidence of salvation coming to his home.

God gives grace to sinners and glory to saints. Jesus didn't offer Zaccheus condemnation for his chicanery, judgment for his deceit, but offered him grace and it changed his life. It was grace all the way when God saved you. Grace is unearned. It is a gift of God.

And it is the greatest gift we have to offer anyone.

Legalistic preachers frustrate the grace of God by turning Christianity into a works project. Salvation is all of grace. Not ours—God's.

I heard this definition of grace, "Grace is the power to do what is right for the sake of Jesus Christ and His kingdom, not the grace that grants me the right to do what I want or feel in pursuit of happiness and peace."

Grace marks the life of the irresistible husband.

Love and grace change people. But grace is the essence of love. It is impossible to say you love if there is no grace given to the one loved.

## SOME NEED GREATER GRACE!

Gene saw Patti's pretty face at the end of a long hallway in an insurance agency where he conducted business on a monthly, and sometimes weekly basis. Upon first glance at the raven-haired beauty, he immediately sensed the Holy Spirit tell him to pray for her. As their business relationship developed, Gene's prayer for Patti developed on his part into a sense of intimacy with her, and an increasing desire to have her as a wife.

Gene had no way of knowing that her roommate was not just a roommate but a lover of five years, the last in a string of many women lovers. Patti had been born into a family of illegitimate children, whose father had disappeared in her early childhood. Her stepfather had been a drunk and abuser. Out of what she considered to be self-defense during one of his drunken rages when she was thirteen, she had pulled a stolen gun on him. Her mother had been forced to make a decision and chose the drunk, turning her thirteen-year-old daughter out onto the streets to fare for herself.

The only "safe" place Patti knew was the apartment of a local heroin dealer, who quickly taught her the ropes of selling, resulting in five separate altercations where a loaded gun was held to her head. It was miraculous she survived long enough to be thrown into a juvenile jail at age 14. There she had her first homosexual encounter, and started a long line of relationships with women who provided her care and comfort as she worked her way into a respectable job in society. Even without an education, Patti grew to command a six-figure income with an office in a Los Angeles skyscraper where she sold specialized insurance premiums.

Patti couldn't stand Gene when she met him. Many men had tried to "pick her up" over the years and she detested them. She knew how to turn on the charm, however, to get the sale, reap the commissions and take home the money to spend on her lover. But Gene was different. His gentle words and many kindnesses haunted her. He asked her to dinners like other men, but never insinuated that something more than dinner was on his mind. He even gave her a Bible and tried to pray with her.

The God that Gene offered Patti was different from anything she'd ever experienced. Unknown to Gene, Patti's relationship with her lover was escalating in its physical abusiveness, and Patti found herself in the bottom of the closet one day, bruised and shivering, and calling out for "the God of Gene" to save her.

After a couple of years of Gene's patient prayers, Patti felt she had to make a move professionally, and she went to work for Gene's company, leaving her lover temporarily. There she was, with the man who made her so uncomfortable, who did things like inviting her out to watch the sunset in the evenings.

One night as they sat in his truck looking down at the lights of the city, Patti heard a voice, which she believes now was the audible voice of God. The voice said, "Tell Gene tonight that you care about him, or I'm going to release him and you'll miss what could have been."

Instantly, Patti turned to Gene, but instead of saying what she knew God had told her to say, she said, "I have a headache, please take me home."

As they descended down the mountain, Patti could not stand the feeling of conviction for her disobedience, and she admitted to Gene that she cared for him and that, whatever she had to do to get Gene's God, she wanted that to be done. Gene led her in a "sinner's prayer" and Patti was converted by grace through faith.

Immediately Gene's eyes were open, and he suddenly realized the woman he had spent three years falling in love with was a lesbian. That night he asked Patti to leave her lover and marry him. She followed his lead blindly, and never saw her former lover again. But that was only the start, not in any way an end.

Gene now had a new Christian to disciple, a new wife to adjust to, and a woman who had just come out of a lesbian, man-hating lifestyle. To say Patti had "rough edges" would be a huge understatement. To top it off, Patti became pregnant, and all her hormones went to war against Gene as well. She constantly struggled with wanting to leave, to walk out on him, and return to her former lifestyle to raise the child alone. Gene struggled with her anger. His deep-seated worry was that after all those years and all his prayer, he had actually married amiss. Submitting himself to God in prayer, Gene prayed the most selfless prayer a husband can pray.

"God," he said, "I don't care if Patti never loves me. But please help her to love You."

Gene told Patti the same, that all he asked of the mother of his child was that she love God, regardless of her feelings for him. After one child, Patti again became pregnant with a second. For the first time, she saw the "escape door" closing. She knew she could live as a single mom with one child, but she no longer felt she could run away with two children to care for.

Patti struggled with how God had "done" bad things to her in her life and how God was "forcing" her to stay with

Gene now. She didn't know how to love a God Who had watched as she was abused and misused without intervening. As Patti worked out her relationship with God, all Gene could do was administer grace. God's grace within him gave him patience. Gene prayed fervently, patiently, and loved her unconditionally. The tirades aimed at him, the nightmares that awakened her, the very hatred in her eyes, he bore as well as he could, believing God for His love to drive out all the conflicts lodged in his wife's heart and spirit.

The Proverb says, "A man's gift makes room for him,"[8] and Gene's gift of grace made room for him in Patti's heart. Patti slowly came to love God more fully, and with that love came a profound respect for her husband. He continued to pray with her, and saw her delivered from oppression, anger, hurt and bitterness in one dramatic encounter after another. Interestingly, her greatest breakthroughs came not in a church service or after hearing a great minister, but in the privacy of their bedroom where Gene's steadfast prayers and obedience to God paved the way for Patti to receive God's grace.

When people meet Gene and Patti today, no one can guess their background. They appear to be a happy couple with a perfect little family. Gene became an anchor to Patti, a healing balm to her troubled heart, a covering to her need for leadership, a faithful friend in the midst of her memories of rejection and abandonment. Patti's demeanor is lively and warm, and when her husband speaks she looks at him with obvious tenderness and love. He set his judgment by his own words and actions toward her, and now he is the recipient of respect and grace from Patti.

Grace, grace—God's grace.

How many times did Gene want to lash out, quit, forget it all, call her names, make fun of her background, and walk out so he could start over again with someone that didn't have the problems he found in Patti. But Gene's knowledge of Jesus changed his mind: "For consider him that endured such contradiction of sinners against himself, lest ye be wearied and faint in your minds."[9]

*The only thing we can truly give anyone is the grace of God in Christ Jesus.* God's grace is our battlefield strategy, our workout regimen, our bonding material, and it bubbles out of us in words that are our power. Grace is the manifestation of love. Grace in everyday decisions, seeing past errors, adapting the tone of our voice, overcoming moods. Grace, originating in prayer, operating through words and actions, is the strength of the man who becomes an irresistible husband.

[1]  Hebrews 11:3
[2]  Matthew 12:36
[3]  Matthew 5:22
[4]  Acts 4:33
[5]  I Corinthians 11:29-30
[6]  I John 5:10 AMP
[7]  Luke 19:8-9 TLB
[8]  Proverbs 18:16
[9]  Hebrews 12:3

## CHAPTER EIGHT

# ABOLISH THE "NO GO ZONE"

The bar owner sued the church across the street after his building burned down. At the trial the two attorneys faced off. The attorney defending the church attacked first, "What makes you think my client had anything to with the destruction of the property? No one ever went there or even near it!"

"They prayed something would happen to close it, and the fire certainly did," the bar owner's attorney said.

"What has that got to do with it burning down?"

"It has everything to do with it."

"How?"

Looking around the packed courtroom, the attorney for the bar owner said, "I guess this bar owner believes in prayer more than the church does!"

"Therefore I say unto you, What things soever ye desire, when ye pray, believe that ye receive them, and ye shall have them."[1]

Prayer changes things! How did Gene overcome the obstacles in his relationship with Patti? The principle he discovered is one I've taught all over the world: Prayer produces intimacy.

Just because you hook up with a woman who later agrees to marry you doesn't mean you instantly have a sense of intimacy and deep connection with her. Far from it. I've been to the Grand Canyon, have crossed many oceans and valleys by air, and I can attest to the fact that the largest gulf in the world, the most deadly chasm of all, is often a six inch strip down the middle of a married couple's bed. The "No Go Zone."

We talk about it, laugh nervously about it, then wonder why adultery is rampant even in church circles. It's no wonder at all.

## REALLY CONNECT!

The biggest hurdle you have to experiencing the fullness of a relationship with your wife is intimacy. The toughest thing for a man to take is rejection. To let down your guard and open your heart is one of the hardest things you'll ever do.

Intimacy is almost completely absent in our world. Parents don't often give it. Sex only promises it. We aren't sure what it is, but we know we want it, yet no one seems to know how to get it. Men and women alike run to movies, hide in books, shield themselves with busy-ness, or obsess over careers or TV shows rather than invest themselves into a relationship that has the potential for true intimacy.

We as men are born with a capacity for intimacy. We were created to be in intimate relationship, and we feel unfulfilled and frustrated when that desire for relationship cannot be satisfied. But just because we are married, and see our spouse as she is while she sees us as we are, this does not automatically create intimacy.

The first step toward intimacy is trust. Trust is extended to the limit of truth and no further.

In the absence of truth, trust has become a vacuous word which gets batted about but rarely realized in our society. The answer to the oft-asked question, "Don't you trust me?" is almost always, "NO!" Until truth is restored in our culture, trust will be absent.

The tool to achieve trust is truth. Each time you and your spouse accept truth, speak truth, love truth, you put a brick in place on the load-bearing wall of your marriage which is called "Trust." As truth is put into place, trust rises. Truth about how much you ate last night, what you bought at the store, where you went after work, what your mother said about your new car. The small issues decide the larger issue. Truth. Truth. Truth.

Truth and trust depend on prayer and love. Once trust is in place, though, prayer changes into a completely different tool. It is so simple, so basic to life, that men pass over it without realizing it holds the answer to their heart's desire for intimacy. *Prayer produces intimacy.*

Prayer is vital to life because it is the place of establishing our relationship with God and our Lord Jesus Christ. The Holy Spirit Himself leads and guides us in prayer. Nothing of eternal value is done in the Kingdom of God without prayer. None are saved without prayer. In all my life, I have never met a saved person who could not tell me of someone they knew who had prayed for them.

Prayer is a place to hide with God. It is a place to secrete yourself with God so He can share His secrets with you. When His secrets are made known we call them "revelations." "But thou, when thou prayest, enter into thy closet, and when thou hast shut thy door, pray to thy Father which is in secret; and thy Father which seeth in secret shall reward thee openly."[2]

Prayer is one of life's major discoveries—a rich fountain of truth. The presence of God is a treasure greater than any other known to man. In the presence of God is fullness of joy, power and wisdom. When the glory of God becomes manifest in our hearts, we experience the awesome wonder of knowing Him. Prayer is the place of true humility, where our humanity bows in humble adoration to divinity. The secret place is where the reality of truth grips the heart, and we know that we know, that we know, that nothing is impossible with God. The only impossibility with God is failure.

In prayer we find God's wondrous will, purpose and plan. We actually pray with portions of the mind of Christ as we pray the will of God. In intimate relationship, reality and truth take hold of our minds and righteousness becomes the force of faith. Known unto God are His secrets and He reveals them to those who hunger and thirst after righteousness. We will never find them or have them until we know the way to the secret place of God.

*Prayer doesn't move God—prayer moves mountains.* Prayer knows no boundaries of space or time. Prayer allows us to go where we have never gone before, to do what we have never done before, so we can be what we have never been before.

In prayer we "go beyond the map."

"Surely the Lord GOD will do nothing, but He revealeth His secret unto His servants the prophets."[3]

## GO BEYOND THE SECRET PLACE

The priests in the Old Testament were instructed to go to the secret place to pray, then come out to minister to the people. In the same way, once you have found the place of prayer privately, you can lead your wife into the secret place with God, where you become intimate with one another and with your Lord together. Nothing is more sacred, more wondrous, more fulfilling, than to share your true heart, and enter into real intimacy with God and with a living person on earth, your wife.

I never get tired of teaching that "prayer produces intimacy" because the truth of it is inexhaustible. This letter from a young man named Sharif says it all.

> I have read your books and attended your meetings for years. I have seen great changes in my life, yet my wife and I still had some problems. I knew what the problem was and I had always avoided doing what needed to be done. My wife and I talked

last week, and in tears she said she was not able to connect with me the way she wanted to. What she wanted was intimacy, and you have taught many times that if a man and his wife want intimacy they must pray together. That is precisely what I had avoided doing.

Seeing my wife in tears, the conviction of the Holy Spirit at that moment caused great sorrow in my heart. I knew this was my fault and no one else's. At that moment I got on my knees in front of my wife and asked her forgiveness for having denied her that intimacy she so craved. She forgave me and we prayed together asking forgiveness of the Lord for neglecting to pray together.

I told her that we would start that very night setting aside time each day to read, study and pray together. We wanted to start small and not make much of a demand on ourselves—not set ourselves up for failure. So we agreed to set aside a half hour at night. Well, God sure performs beyond any expectations. That first night we spent three hours reading, talking and praying, and only stopped because we had to get some sleep. I learned more about my wife that night than I had in the last three years. I noticed that when we went to bed she drifted off to sleep holding my hand. I was amazed. I climbed out of bed after she was asleep and got on my face before God to beg His forgiveness again for having cut that blessing out of our life for so long.

Now I feel like I am a newlywed again. I am learning more of my wife's desires and needs, and her WISDOM than ever before. We have grown more together in days than in the last year. We are truly excited to spend time together now. Only days ago we were fighting and accusing one another of being the problem. Where we used to sit in front of the TV, we now spend looking into each other's eyes and talking and praying and reading and discussing God's Word. When I used to tell her things I knew in the Word, she would say I was 'pontificating.' Now I see great expectation in her eyes when I open the Bible as I share with her what she really needs and not what I feel like she needs to change. There's a big difference.

I have read your books and am faithful to my church. But all of this means nothing without prayer. By praying with my wife I have become a better minister to her. I am already developing strategies to help our children, and to bring the family together in prayer. I am sure that there are a lot of men out there just like me who are putting it off because they just don't know what they are missing. We as men need to continue to rise up and be the leaders and ministers in our homes. Thank you for teaching me how.

For years Sharif heard it, read it, saw it, but didn't do it. It's not the knowing, it's the doing that counts. The irresistible husband prays with his wife. The old axiom is true, "The family that prays together stays together."

Prayer is easier and less expensive than divorce, with none of the negative consequences that come with it. Prayer is better than a diamond bracelet, for with prayer you give her yourself, not "things." Prayer changes you, not God. Prayer is the place of exchange—the lesser for the greater.

## THE ANTIDOTE TO ADULTERY

Intimacy, not good intentions, is the antidote to adultery. The reason God said, "thou shalt not commit adultery,"[4] is because of the propensity of fallen human nature to commit such sins against each other.

It has been said that adultery is responsible for 50% of all human misery. King David knew of this when he said, "My sin is ever before me."[5] His adultery with a married woman, Bathsheba, was an act of murder against the covenant of marriage. He then literally committed murder, killing Bathsheba's husband to cover up his actions.

I have no statistics to prove it, but from my observations, I believe one great cause of the rise of the divorce rate is the rise of premarital sex. We seem to have forgotten as a society that sex was intended for marriage, and instead are bombarded with sexual images in advertising, in clothing stores, in our music, everywhere. Even if we turn off the TV, don't read the newspapers, and refuse to go to movies, we still cannot escape the sexual images in the culture in which we live.

As a result, teenagers lose their virginity as a matter of routine, not scandal, and couples sleep together before marriage, which sets them up later for not regarding the marriage bed as sacred.

We as men must accept responsibility for our actions. In the Garden of Eden, Adam refused to accept responsibility for his actions, and brought death into the world. But the "Last Adam"—the Lord Jesus Christ—accepted responsibility for the sins of the entire world, and brought eternal life to swallow up death. Men must aspire to be as the Last Adam and accept responsibility for their own actions, for the actions of their family, and for the world for which Christ died.

The man who impregnates a woman, and refuses the responsibility of the child she bears is the epitome of immaturity. The man who impregnates a woman, and insists she has an abortion, is the epitome of escapist wimpiness. To take the life-giving womb, and turn it into a tomb, is to create a mockery of God's creation of life. To think you can do that, and then sit in church and ask for God's blessings without repentance, is to doom yourself from ever reaching your maximum fulfillment as a man.

I've taught all over the world that every man has one gift he can give one time to one person in one lifetime. *One gift, one time, one person, one lifetime!* It's called virginity. God uses virginity to establish the covenant of marriage between men and women. When the marriage is consummated on the wedding night, and the husband and wife are together in sexual intimacy for the first time, the natural shedding of blood is the sign of the holy covenant of marriage, and the reflection on earth of the heavenly covenant God made with mankind through the shedding of Christ's blood. There is nothing lewd, lustful, or laughable about the covenant act of marriage. It is honorable, praiseworthy, and highly valuable when entered into with sobriety, sincerity and selectivity.

When a man is a virgin before marriage, and remains faithful to his wife throughout marriage, the AIDS epidemic stops, sexually transmitted disease no longer threatens young men and women, abortion is no longer an option, illegitimacy is not an issue and, I believe, the divorce rate drops.

God made sex good. Man, through sin, makes it bad.

*Love is the desire to benefit others even at the expense of self, because love desires to give. Lust is the desire to benefit self even at the expense of others because lust desires to get.* Lust is insatiable, but love is easily satisfied. Lust is a counterfeit for love. Sex was made for loving and giving, not for lusting and getting.

God invested His love in us at creation, but it changed to lust when Adam was expelled from the Garden of Eden. God is love. Satan is the progenitor of lust.

Lust is the motivation for extramarital affairs, not love. Men know it, but complain about their wives in order to justify their own lusts. Women claim when they are tempted it is due to love, and ignore the obvious fact that it is lust. Remember, when we succumb to our lust, sin is conceived, and sin brings forth death. Nothing is worth the murder of a marriage, and nothing can repair a broken marriage covenant.

Most marriage counselors will tell you the same, that when a couple comes in for help for a damaged marriage, the marriage is generally already dead. There is no provision in all of Scripture for repairing a broken covenant. The only thing that can be done is to create a new covenant. That's why I tell men they don't need a rejuvenated or restored marriage, they need a brand new marriage—a resurrected marriage.

## TALK TO YOUR WIFE!

The wild "cajun" preacher, Jesse DuPlantis, tells a story of a man who took him aside in a meeting and admitted he was having a problem with lusting other women.

"No problem at all," Jesse said smiling, then he called over the man's wife. "Your husband here is having a problem lusting other women!"

The man turned shades of red Jesse had never seen before, and Jesse claims the next time he saw the man, he declared himself "cured." I've never used that method in dealing with men, but certainly I've seen a tremendous freedom come to men who face their problems head-on, and learn to confide in their wives.

Rejecting truth about ourselves, sloughing it off, pretending it doesn't exist, not admitting it, refusing to deal with the issues, or accepting it as part of our "manhood" leaves us fair game to *be* overcome by what Jesus said He gave us *power* to overcome. Jesus said, "all power in heaven and earth is given" unto Him.[6] As we abide in Christ, and His Word abides in us, there is nothing impossible with God.[7] It may be impossible with men, but not God. No sin is too great, no wound too deep, no obstacle too high for God to save us from, and deliver us into a whole new life.

Men are willing to fight, wrestle, box, or clash in football, but not struggle until the battle is won in the spirit. We war against the flesh and the devil. "There hath no temptation taken you but such as is common to man: but God is faithful, who will not suffer you to be tempted above that ye are able; but will with the temptation also make a way to escape, that ye may be able to bear it."[8] The way of escape is not to run from it, but to deal with it head-on.

Because I spent my married life developing a relationship of true intimacy with my wife, when I felt tempted or overwhelmed by the sex-saturated society in which I live, I would tell my wife. Obviously I told her with wisdom. I didn't say, "So and so looks mighty good to me," but rather, "I'm struggling, will you pray for me?" If you've built trust and intimacy into your marriage, your spouse will be your closest friend and best ally.

Many times I would be ministering in some far-off city in a hotel room, lonely and feeling tempted, when I would call my wife and she would pray for me. She literally at times had me place the receiver of the phone on my chest and she prayed over my heart, over my life, interceding for my very spirit. When her body gave in to a disease and she departed my life to enter Heaven, I missed the intimacy and comfort of those telephone calls.

## THE TORMENT OF THE CONSEQUENCE IS UNBEARABLE

I was once in Hawaii where I'd just preached, and now had a couple of days in a hotel alone before going home. Hearing the sounds of laughter and music drifting up to the open hotel room window, suddenly it didn't seem enough to have the fresh ocean breeze, the fern-lined walking trails and a delightful beach outside my window. Suddenly it seemed as if I would give anything to join those people and have the company of a young woman. After thirty years of marriage, the temptation still came.

As I sat in the hotel room, with my conscience struggling between right and wrong, my will wavering, my spirit fighting for morality, a sentence came to me. Men who have heard that sentence which I've preached all over the world still today remind me of it because it has helped keep them through many a temptation. The sentence is, *"The torment of the temptation to sin is nothing to compare with the torment of the consequence of that sin."* I could have lost my marriage, my family, my ministry, my influence, my future, in one careless act in one moment of weakness. Stupid!

The righteousness we have in Jesus Christ makes sex good in a Christian marriage. The man who desires to be an irresistible husband puts away the uncleanness of the world to allow the fresh waters of the Holy Spirit to flow through him, and accepts the riches of what is godly, pure and holy in his bedroom. The irresistible husband is a man after God's own heart.

He's not a perfect man, just a maturing man.

His wife knows he will not expose her to the agony of shame, loss and loneliness—to the degradation of hidden sins that are exposed. His wife knows he is true to God and to her.

He is a man who is faithful—and faithful to repent.

In his bed the irresistible husband does not have a sex partner, but a heart-sharer. He has abolished the "No Go Zone" through prayer, truthfulness, trust, true love and that greatest element: true intimacy. He is a husband who truly "connects."

[1] Mark 11:24
[2] Matthew 6:6
[3] Amos 3:7
[4] Exodus 20:14
[5] Psalm 51:3
[6] Matthew 28:18
[7] Luke 1:37
[8] I Corinthians 10:13

## Chapter Nine

# Join the REAL Gentlemen's Club

Stealing is trespassing on another's right of possession. It is taking their right and making it yours, violating their ownership. It is a form of anarchy, creating disorder and confusion. Legally, stealing is called larceny. Technically, it is simply taking something that belongs to someone else—anything.

For example, not tithing is stealing from God.[1] Not giving an honest day's work is stealing from an employer. Not giving correct wages is stealing from an employee. Creating debt without having the ability to pay is also a form of stealing. And, taking what belongs to your wife and family is theft as well.

"Let the husband render unto the wife due benevolence: and likewise also the wife unto the husband. The wife hath not power of her own body, but the husband: and likewise also the husband hath not power of his own body, but the wife."[2]

When you take what is your wife's and give it to your car, your friends, your work or even your ministry, you steal from your wife and defraud her. The passage from the Apostle Paul speaks of sexually not withholding our bodies, but an irresistible husband does not withhold his body for any reason from what rightfully belongs to his wife or children.

## Gentlemen—Start Your Marriages!

The mail I receive from women tells me many are frustrated with men's indifference to the common courtesies of life. Many feel unfulfilled in their uniqueness because it is not recognized by their husbands. They want to be treated like ladies, not buddies. Some feel their husbands want them to compete with our culture's "sex goddesses," yet the men exempt themselves from physical fitness. These are the kind of men who look at "Car and Track" magazine and think about a trade-in for their "dream machine," then think the same with a Playboy magazine and their wives!

Our culture has shortened the word "gentlemen" to "men." "Gentlemen" are almost extinct except for the floor of the Congress, on some restroom doors, and some "Gentlemen's Clubs" which is a misnomer of the lowest degree. Yet the truest Christian is the finest gentleman. In every sense, the word "gentleman" is a term of dignity, worth, value, and character, and is the designation for the real man who willingly gives his wife her due.

*Women simply want husbands who act like gentlemen!* Gentlemanliness is displayed in thought, appearance, manners, hygiene, speech, habits, and character traits.

### Thought

Gentlemen are thoughtful because they train their minds to think of how to serve others. "Your care for others is the measure of your greatness." Christ not only said it, but proved it in the sacrifice of Himself for the sins of the world. Men prove it in their willingness to sacrifice themselves for the welfare of their family, employees or fellow man. Jesus said, "He that would be Lord let him be the servant of all." A man is only qualified to lead to the degree he is willing to serve. Serving is not servitude. Serving is voluntary, servitude is involuntary. A servant's heart is better than a ruler's mentality.

### Appearance, Manners, Hygiene

Gentlemen groom their appearance and demeanor, adjusting how they come across to others. Christian men recognize their role as an "ambassador of Jesus Christ." They know that to win others to their God, including their own families, they first must win others to themselves. Gentlemen creatively improve relationships rather than taking others for granted and trying only to maintain what once was. The Bible says, "kindness makes a man attractive," so a gentleman's grooming is internal as well as external.

## Speech

Gentlemen know that out of the abundance of their hearts their mouths speak, so they keep their hearts pure before God and guard the words of their mouths.[3] They are totally unlike "bubbas" who spew from the mouth, wanting everyone to think they have four aces, when all they have is a pair of deuces.

## Habits

Gentlemen build self-discipline by developing good habits. They know that meekness is not weakness, but is the ability to control one's own spirit. Gentleness is the true sign of strength, as King David said to God, "Thy gentleness has made me great."[4]

## Character Traits

Gentlemen know they have to build into their character Christlike attributes starting with faithfulness, which is the cornerstone of character. Because their character is good, their name is good. "A good name is rather to be had than riches," the Proverb says.[5] Rather than defrauding his wife by robbing her of a good name, a gentleman gives his wife a name she can bear with pride.

## TELEVISION IS A THIEF

As to the women who write to me, by far the biggest complaint, next to the rise of Internet pornography, is that wives and children simply cannot get their husband's or father's attention. "The number one problem in marriage today is not lust, it is television," one woman wrote. "My husband is glued to the TV. He never reads his Bible or prays, but watches TV. I wish it would blow up!" She stopped short of saying, "and him with it!"

*What is submitted to in life grows stronger, what is resisted grows weaker.* Submit to the lusts of television—for food, sex, material goods, wealth, other women—and those desires will grow stronger. Submit to the Word of God and the needs of your family, and your character will grow, as will your relationships.

Television is a totally discourteous, inanimate intrusion into personal relationships, and a thief that robs time from others. It also robs a man from his ability to develop into a true gentleman, an irresistible husband, and a father in whom his children take pride. Often we men become so set in our habits, we don't realize we have options.

"Give attendance to reading" is an injunction given to all men.[6] The loss of the love of reading, the habit of reading, and the pursuit of reading is the gain in the realm of ignorance. The common man stops the habit of study or reading after his schooling. The uncommon man turns off the television to continue to read and study all through life.

Gavin and Patti MacLeod, of "Love Boat" fame are well known for their outspoken views on marriage, having been reunited from a nasty divorce themselves. They read to each other in the evenings to promote their unity and give them common ground from which to communicate.

Pro-Bowl and Superbowl winning Reggie White was saved from divorce when he and Sara read a book aloud together during a road trip many years ago. Reading to each other is not for wimps, but for men who are willing to face truths they otherwise would not know, and for courageous men who are ready to act on what they read!

## Reading Makes You Irresistible

The greatest sight in all the world is not Victoria Falls in Zimbabwe nor Niagara Falls in America, not the Sphinx nor the Taj Mahal, not the Grand Canyon nor the Swiss Alps, but the sight of a man reading the Bible to his family. A man reading to or with his child is a sight to behold.

A father misrepresents God to his children when he leaves the education entirely to the mother. When a child is taught and trained only by Mother, he or she wants to grow up to be a man "just like mom." Mothers resent being left to fend for themselves, raising children while the father sits in the next room glued to a television program. Reading is the easiest ingredient in child development that bonds parent to child. Caring enough for your children to read to or with them will make you great in their eyes and in your wife's eyes.

The practice of reading develops the power of concentration, encourages creative thinking, broadens understanding, increases sharpness of mind and enjoyment of life. Reading to children develops their power of concentration so they'll do better in school. Keeping the mind active is an agent against aging. If you and your children simply watch television, your minds will be more sluggish. As a result, they'll mature slower and you'll age faster.

*Men do not own what they possess, they are only stewards.* The three basic responsibilities of any steward is to guide, guard and govern. Those are the three areas of responsibility of a man with his family. In practical terms this means to direct, protect and correct. In relationship, it is to nourish, cherish and admonish. Fathers who are godly stewards are the earth's and a family's greatest blessing. Teaching children to be good stewards of their minds is a lesson taught by example.

Reading is an art form, and every man can be an artist. I've had men tell me, "But I don't read that good." That's no surprise. If you don't read, you won't read "good." The only way you'll read "good" is if you read! It's so simple we miss it. Television, CD's, audio cassettes, are all technological marvels, but not if they usurp the skill of reading.

## SAVE CHILDREN FROM IGNORANCE

*Reading is the most inexpensive thing a man can do, and not doing it is the most expensive.* Reading the Bible to your children is the most inexpensive thing you can do, but the most expensive thing you don't do.

The Bible says it was through ignorance that men crucified Christ, and it is through ignorance that men are destroyed. "My people are destroyed for lack of knowledge: because thou hast rejected knowledge, I will also reject thee, that thou shalt be no priest to me: seeing thou hast forgotten the law of thy God, I will also forget thy children."[7]

Ignorance in its most common form is simply a lack of knowledge. Failure to instruct and implant truth into children's minds and hearts leaves them ignorant, and the father liable before God. However, if you school them in the Word, will and ways of God, and they reject it, they are liable for their own consequences.

*"Children will not always listen to you, but they will always imitate you."* The example set is not in the words that are spoken, but in the deeds done as a pattern to be followed. It is not the father's responsibility to make all his children's decisions for them, but to let them see him make his. Setting the pattern by taking time to read engenders good study habits. The TV generation that is taught to learn in "sound bites" is easily led astray and has no concept of where to look for real answers when the inevitable crises arise.

Too often, fathers try to do the work of the Word in their children's lives. Fathers wait until there is a crisis, then try to tell the children what the Bible says about it, which breeds resentment in the heart of the child toward God. "The yoke you wear determines the burden you bear."[8] Your yoke is what you believe and what you believe determines the burden you carry in life. Reading the Word to your children yokes them to truth which creates the lightest burden. It provides them with a platform from which to build their own relationship with God over a lifetime, not just during a crisis.

Reading the Bible also teaches your children to love and respect wisdom. To hold God's Word in our hands, study it, learn from it, apply it, is a treasure made possible because of a few real men who recognized and respected wisdom. William Tyndale was strangled by a hangman and burned at the stake in 1535 for translating the Scriptures into common language. John Cranmer and John Rogers followed his fate trying to preserve God's Word for you and your family. Less than five hundred years ago the Geneva Bible was made available to the public. These men fought and died for the right to read the Bible, and to give you its truths today. They gave their lives for what they counted more dear than life itself. Yet we take the Bible so casually. Few believers today ever read the Bible in its entirety. Instead we base our lives on Sunday morning readings and three-minute prayers.

"Home is the school of first instruction." Parenting is the basic societal art form. Training is teaching by example, and to train up a child properly is to set an example for them to follow. "Follow me as I follow Christ," is the pattern for fathering.[9] What is taught in the home by word and deed determines the culture of a nation or people. No wonder our children have learned to watch television, when millions of fathers believe it is the sovereign right of men to live with a remote control secured in their hands.

## Develop A Taste For The Best Life

"Just as my mouth tastes good food, so my mind tastes truth when I hear it."[10] Teaching your children to love truth by reading to them gives them a taste for the best life. The best is when you can do no better, and nothing can be better than the Word of God.

Words are power, and life and death are in the power of the tongue.[11] We live on the basis of the words others have spoken to us that we have received into our lives, or the words we have spoken which have become the basis of our belief and conduct. Reading the Bible to your children gives them words with which to create a world for themselves that is filled with truth, grace, liberty, wisdom, righteousness, and honor. What a life! What a legacy.

Public reading of God's Word was once done religiously in synagogues and churches. It taught people to listen and learn. Today in most churches it is uncommon to hear more than a scripture text for a sermon. *Absence of knowledge of the Word leaves people scripturally illiterate.*

Absence of public reading has allowed secular humanists to legislate reading the Word to private practice. Mental unhealthiness in America is mostly derived from the lack of knowledge of the Word of God. It's no wonder people are disturbed. When so many are living on the advice of psychics, astrologists, psychologists, watching unhealthy people defend their sick predilections on talk shows, putting trust in lying leadership, and believing paranormal phenomena to determine their choices in life, it's a marvel they do as well as they do.

We preach and pray for revival, yet what might help most is if we simply found a time and place for public reading of the Bible. We have a National Prayer Day, but a National Bible Day where the Bible is read in every city would help even more. The Word does the work!

Reading the Bible to the family lets the Word do the work rather than parents trying to "work the Word."

The irresistible husband is above all else a lover of God's Word. He does not steal time from the Word and from his family by giving it to television or hobbies or friends. He freely gives his family attention, and leads them in paths of righteousness by allowing them to see him walk that path himself.

[1] Malachi 3:8
[2] I Corinthians 7:3-4
[3] Matthew 12:34
[4] Psalm 18:35
[5] Proverbs 22:1
[6] I Timothy 4:13
[7] Hosea 4:6
[8] Matthew 11:29-32
[9] I Corinthians 11:1
[10] Job 12:11 TLB
[11] Proverbs 18:21

# Chapter Ten

# Adopt a Guide to Life

For most of us, no one ever gave us the opportunity to learn a structure for life that really works. No wonder we steal from others, when we don't know that the structure we accidentally built, based on what we saw in others, robs our wives and children of our time and attention. Structure determines how life will be lived. Structure also provides for spontaneity and makes allowances for mistakes. If a basic structure exists, we can do something out of the ordinary or make a big blunder without everything else falling apart.

Structure must be built on wisdom. Wisdom is vital to everything we do in life. "Wisdom is the principle thing, therefore get wisdom and with all thy getting, get understanding."[1] Wisdom provides a man with the ability to gain everything he will ever need. "Wisdom gives: a long, good life, riches, honor, pleasure, peace."[2] Wisdom has incomparable value, more than the most valuable jewels.[3] The man who knows right from wrong and has good judgment and common sense is happier than the man who is immensely rich.

"If any of you lack wisdom, let him ask of God, that giveth to all men liberally, and upbraideth not; and it shall be given him."[4] God promises to give you wisdom IF you ask. The only condition for receiving wisdom is asking.

Wisdom emanates from, and originates in, Jesus Christ. "But of him are ye in Christ Jesus, who of God is made unto us wisdom, and righteousness, and sanctification, and redemption."[5]

Theology is only helpful if it can be lived. If your theology has no practical application, it is not good theology. If your

102

belief in God gives you no ability to live on earth, but only promises a future blessing in heaven, then it is an incomplete knowledge of God. So let me give you some insights, understanding, good judgment and wisdom that if followed can help you avoid mistakes, pitfalls, and the grief they cause. It will give you the ability to build a structure that allows you to live together in marriage and enjoy a great life.

## Your Guide To Daily Living

**Number One:** *Set your personal calendar before your business calendar.*

Give your family preeminence. Don't sacrifice your family on the altar of your business or ministry. Your family comes first, and must not be left as the dregs of what you didn't give to others. Because they have committed their lives to you, and their lives depend on you, they must be respected with taking first place in your life. Too many men set their business calendar, then find they don't have time to do what the family wants, or the family cannot do what they want. This makes the family feel like second-class citizens.

Your Bible is the most important book in your possession. Yet two books reveal more about your true passions—your date book and your check book. Look where any man invests his time and money, and you'll know the man. Both reveal the priorities of relationships in your life. Your calendar is your "bible" for family living.

**Number Two:** *Try never to cancel family plans.*

This is the corollary to Number One. Too many men plan things then cancel them either out of business priorities, personal preferences, or a desire for something else without the family. Canceling family plans disappoints children, discourages your wife's faith in you and, if not corrected, can degenerate into resentment as a result of disappointment. Resentment, if not corrected, can degenerate into rebellion.

This is especially important for those with great work responsibilities, such as managers, medical men or ministers, and for those with great circles of people around them, such as salesmen or sportsmen. You married your wife and had your family regardless of what those around you did or said, so now you have to make them the priority regardless of what those around you do or say.

Canceling family plans gives priority to something other than the family. Children don't understand it. Wives put up with it, but it will never be erased from their minds or emotions. Avoid family crisis by keeping your word and carrying out your plans. Your word is your bond. You make covenant when you give your word. Not to perform it breaks covenant with whom it is given.

**Number Three:** *Do not let your business, ministry or hobby become an idol, mistress or an excuse.*

Make sure your wife knows you have greater affection for her, so she won't see something else as your mistress and her competition. Don't make your wife compete for your affection. She was created to be your completion, not your competition. Let her complete—not compete. Just as you can't have two heads on one body, you can't have two loves without giving priority to one. Make her the one.

**Number Four:** *Do not make your secretary or female colleague an "office wife."*

Secretaries and female associates who admire the qualities of a gentleman which they see in you may become willing to do whatever you want, adapt to your whims, and meet any need you seem to have. They can develop an intimacy with your work habits, peculiarities, likes and dislikes, and take on the role of your protector. They'll learn how you like your coffee and when, and even what you want to give people as gifts, so they can send them. When they know more about you and take care of you more than your wife—STOP!—you've gone too far. When the only difference between a work associate and a wife is that the wife gives you sex, it's likely that pretty soon the work associate may do that, too.

If such a woman feels a man is misunderstood by his wife, look out! The beleaguered man with the misunderstanding wife creates the "sympathetic sister syndrome" which is anything but. Compensation is always to come in the form of a paycheck not a bedcheck. Likewise, you must not counsel women, and be sucked into the sympathetic syndrome yourself. "Let the aged women teach the younger," is more than a Biblical imperative. It is inspired common sense! Keep yourself pure. If you become a savior to a woman, you'll create an image in her mind that is hard to resist—for her and for you—particularly if your wife doesn't share that view!

*Number Five: Take periodic honeymoons.*

Make time together with your wife uniquely personal. A honeymoon can be just a weekend, or even an overnight stay, if quality time and affection are given. Just pay attention to each other to replenish your relationship.

Too many men take a job, marry, have children, get promoted, and everything they do with their wives is through the children or the business. Don't just take her on a business trip and leave her in a hotel room, making her a prisoner while you work. You might think you're killing two birds with one stone, when in fact you're a dead duck!

Your wife may want to escape *from* the job, routine or children, but she wants to escape *to* her husband. Don't mistake her desire for release and relief as a desire to get away from you. Her desire for sleep, rest and quietness with the ability to simply read and dine in a relaxed atmosphere is not her sign that she wants to get away from you. She wants to be with you, be intimate, have a relationship, but she doesn't always want to have it when somebody else has to be accommodated. She wants *you.*

If she does accompany you on a business outing of any kind, recognize that she won't be receiving the accolades and appreciation others heap on you as she stands in shadows unnoticed and unattended. When conversing with and receiving compliments from others, include your wife in them by introducing her and bringing her close to you to share in them. She will love you for giving her identity and value.

Don't sacrifice creativity at the expense of maintenance. In other words, the new garage door opener (maintenance) may have to wait another month in order to take her to a local hotel's weekend special for two (creativity). It is harder to maintain than it is to obtain. Be creative in doing what pleases your wife to maintain a vital relationship.

**Number Six:** *Have regularly scheduled times together.*

The three cardinal rules for success in real estate are "location, location, location." The three cardinal rules for maintaining a strong marriage are "date her, date her, date her." Dating doesn't stop when you get married, it just ripens and deepens.

The dinner hour on a date is not a time of sitting silently at the table thinking about other matters, but a time of finding out what she is thinking, how she is feeling and what she likes. You can always tell the married couples in a restaurant because they're not talking. Surely there is some fascinating thing in your wife's day which you have not yet allowed her to tell you. Stay current! She wants to feel unique. When you date her, it restores to her that sense of uniqueness she found in courtship that caused her to marry you in the first place.

*Number Seven: Keep your personal devotional life vital.*

Private philosophy determines public performance. You don't read the Bible to fulfill a quota on a reading chart, but to hear it. Clothe yourself with God's Word daily. Faith comes by hearing the Word, not having heard before.[6] Reading makes the Word present tense rather than past. It is not what you *have* read, but what you *are* reading that matters.

God is the essential person in your relationship with your wife. Adam and Eve had a third person intrude into their relationship and take the place of God. The devil ruined their relationship with God, and the rest is history.

God made man responsible for every decision in the home—whether he makes it or not. Your wife loves to have her husband be the spiritual leader. When he is the spiritual leader in the home, she accepts him in leadership in other areas of life. Pray for each member of your family at least once daily.

*Number Eight: Pray with your wife.*

Prayer produces intimacy. You become intimate with the One to Whom you pray, for whom you pray and with whom you pray. Your wife is the greatest protection you have. Prayer gives you the opportunity to share your needs and have her pray for and with you. If trouble comes, she can empathize and intercede for you. It's more common than not for a man to be kept from trouble because of a wife's prayers.

*Number Nine: Relationship precedes ministry.*

Jesus said in His "Sermon on the Mount" that if you have ought against someone, go to them and make it right and then come and bring your gift to the altar. He means, "relationship precedes ministry." Your ministry of work at the church, of giving, of trying to help others, is only as effective as the relationship you have with your wife. Without a deep, personal, intimate relationship with her, your ministry can suffer or die.

Before Abraham was given the responsibility to be the "father of the family of faith" on earth, God proved him as the father of his own earthly family. His ability to lead a family was the one, single, solid reason for God's confidence in Abraham, to give him the stewardship of the family of faith.[7] This is why Paul writes saying that if you cannot lead your own family, you're not qualified to lead the church.[8]

**Number Ten:** *Give your wife and family love and value.*

It is vital that you not only give your wife love, but that you establish her value in her own eyes. Too many men slight their wives, and let the children do so by not establishing the true value that she has in his eyes and in theirs.

When I left the pastorate to begin the ministry to men around the world, my wife stepped out of the place of leadership, authority and high visibility. She had enjoyed the esteem and recognition, as well as the affection of every member of that congregation. She had been the finest pastor's wife that they had ever known. Now Nancy remained home to take care of the family and our finances. She no longer had high visibility, with esteem and affection flowing toward her, or relationships that were intimate and blessed, but was alone and working unseen. It was up to me to show her the value she really had.

For one, I gave her income for what she did as treasurer, and made sure she knew it was hers to do with as she wanted. It showed two things—that I loved her and that she had value.

Secondly, I began to call her "the loveliest lady in the land." It caught on and others began to call her the same. Her license plate rim said it. Others wrote to her with that title. She became known worldwide by that descriptive title. It fit!

Nancy's importance came back to her when others in the ministry around the world saw in her a unique and wonderful woman and gave her their esteem.

Your children need the same. You show them love by the willingness of giving yourself to them. They may not understand the meaning of money, but they do understand the meaning of time. You show them value by giving them time. Children who do not have time with their father feel cheated and valueless. They often become frustrated but don't know why. It's because their worth has been taken from them instead of being established for them. Give them value—with your money, sacrifice to support them, your time, and also compliments. Make your children rich with the value you give them from commendation and affirmation.

**Number Eleven:** *Don't make your wife a beggar, an employee or an appendage.*

As a corollary to the previous activity, whatever you give must be in appreciation for your wife's sacrifices or efforts. When your wife has to ask you for every penny that she wants to spend, get your approval, or somehow appeal to you for money to take care of things, you make her a beggar. Giving your wife money only when she does something that you approve of, or are pleased with, makes her your employee. The Bible says she is a "joint heir" and should share equally in the rewards that come from your labors together. Most women work outside the home because they want to make sure they have income to produce a better life for the family. Failure to recognize her contribution is plain selfishness.

On the other hand, if your wife buys the Christmas gifts for your business, sets up the Board meetings, helps with sales leads, types your reports at home, she should be paid for it. "Don't muzzle the ox that treads out the grain."[9] "The workman is worthy of his hire."[10] My wife's value was established. She didn't have to beg me for money.

Some men make their wives an appendage by dragging them around without ever establishing their value. This used to be prevalent among preachers and politicians whose wives just seemed to be part of the baggage they brought with them. Wrong! She is an integral part of your life, ministry, and career, and when you treat her as such, your constituency, crew or congregation will treat her likewise.

*Number Twelve: Don't make your wife a scapegoat.*

Faultfinding is not a virtue. It's a sin and God hates it. Don't make your wife the scapegoat for your mistakes by blaming her for things you've done wrong. When you suffer the consequences for a bad decision, she's not the scapegoat you can blame and shame so you can be free from your own guilt. Jesus took our sins upon Himself and became our scapegoat. You can lay them on Jesus and He'll forgive you. But laying them on your wife makes it difficult for her to forgive you, and if she ever stops, God help you.

*Number Thirteen: Set times for family council.*

Now we get beyond marriage into family living. The best favor you can do for yourself is learn the principle, "What people do not understand they are against." Humans are negative by nature, so it is easier for us to say "no," than to say, "yes." To get good cooperation, you need good understanding. Thoroughly explain when you'll get the new car, discover what is liked and disliked, discuss vacation plans, and make clear why Junior can't have Tommy Hilfiger jeans this year. Go over the calendar. Read a passage of scripture. Pray. Talking about issues at family council on a regular basis gives good understanding and develops good relationships. Happy campers are the best kind.

*Number Fourteen: Children are not responsible for their parents' problems.*

Children can never do anything about problems that exist solely between you and your wife, or her parents, or your boss, or the argument you have with your neighbor down the street. Most financial difficulties need not be discussed with the children either. If the family is going to cut spending together as a group project, terrific, explain it that way at family council. If the children are going to put coins in a jar to save for the vacation to Disneyland, wonderful. But when they're not old enough to bear the responsibility for matters that belong only to the parents, you overburden them by letting them know those problems exist. If they're old enough to sense something is going on, don't let it "leak" to them, but develop an age-appropriate way of discussing such issues at a specially-called family council.

*Number Fifteen: Knowledge requires responsibility.*

Here's another corollary. The rule of thumb is: Never burden the children with something they can do nothing about. Knowledge of the financial condition of the family means the child shares the responsibility of the parents. If there is nothing a child can do, that is the parent's, not the child's, responsibility. Don't make others responsible for how you feel—especially not your children at a tender age.

I'll never forget some years ago as I concluded preaching in Pennsylvania, a couple of men brought a gentleman up for prayer for his children who were backslidden. The Spirit of God rose up in me and I looked at the man and said, "Where do you go to church?" He bowed his head. I said, "Who's your pastor?" He lowered his head a little lower. The Spirit of God showed me exactly what happened to his children.

"Sir," I said. "I can't pray for your children's salvation because you yourself don't have a church home and you don't have a pastor. The truth is, you left the church out of disagreement with the pastor and you talked badly about him in your home. When you talked about the pastor at home, who represents the headship of Christ, you undermined your children's relationship with Christ. I can't pray for them to be saved, I can only pray for you to repent and make it right with your children. Until you do, it will be hard for them to trust God."

Don't make your children responsible for problems that you alone can solve!

*Number Sixteen: Try never to disagree in front of the children.*

The principles are "agreement produces power," and "disagreement results in powerlessness." When you disagree with your wife in the home, you lose authority over the children. When parents disagree openly, children know about it, resent it, and will eventually rebel against the parents for it. Don't let your children hear you argue, but work it out with your wife privately, then present a united front. Sons and daughters have run away from home and from God because of arguments and even violence in the home. It's terrible to have to say, worse to know about it, and worse still to live through.

*Number Seventeen: Don't make your children an example to other kids.*

Let your children grow up with freedom of expression. Freedom of expression is not license. It doesn't mean that they get to do anything they want to do. It simply means they have the freedom and latitude to express themselves and develop naturally, not unnaturally. I've seen Christians compare their children's behavior with that of others. If that happened, and you suffered from home life but came back to faith in God, then for His sake don't repeat the mistakes of your parents. Stop it with your children's generation.

*Number Eighteen: Both you and your wife continue your education.*

Don't outgrow each other, but rather grow together. Study is a lifelong pursuit. Progress by continuing your studies, together or separately, all your lives. Growth will occur in both of you, and in the family, but you don't want to outgrow each other.

When a wife works to put her husband through college, he graduates with a good degree, obtains a position with promotions, while she has sacrificed for his benefit, he needs to help her. It's her turn.

As he climbs the corporate ladder while she takes care of the home and family, she may become ill at ease with those in his company. When social inequality exists, he can easily think he's better off with someone else. It is far too common a scenario that although she paid the price to make him what he is, he forgets as he enjoys the fruit of her labors, and never helps her in return. A slack sense of gratitude, little appreciation, with no sacrifice on his part, but all on hers, is the characteristic of a male, but not a man.

Helping her define and achieve her goals is as satisfactory to you as achieving your own—if you really love her.

**Number Nineteen**: *Recreation is vital to inspiration.*

A rested mind is receptive to new ideas. Take time to exercise your bodies and get oxygen to your brain cells. Enjoy recreational pursuits together rather than separately if you can find something you mutually enjoy. She may prefer playing tennis to watching a baseball game, so find something recreationally that you and she enjoy together. Don't make her always bend to your will. Learning each other's tastes and hobbies helps build unity. Enjoying things together, resting together, being refreshed together, allows for excellence in relationship together.

**Number Twenty**: *Make your home your castle.*

A man's home is his place of comfort, solace, refuge, refreshing, not a place of tension, strife and discourse of troubles. Show your wife that when she treats you like a king, you'll respond by treating her like a queen. Headstrong and beautiful Sarah willingly called her husband Abraham "lord." Serving is the path to lordship.

### Number Twenty-One: *Help her organize her home.*

Women have a "nesting instinct" whereby they find their uniqueness in their homes. If the wife is the Chief Operation Officer of the home, then the man is the Chief Executive Officer. Whatever skills you use to organize and run your job or business, you must offer to help her in her home. A disorganized home, or your own procrastination to help her, will create tension among all the family members. Organization is vital to good relationships.

"How wonderful it is, how pleasant, when brothers live in harmony!"[11] The same could certainly be said for married couples!

### Number Twenty-Two: *Don't second-guess your wife publicly.*

Correction is a private matter. Compliments are a matter for public record. To transpose those two is to create problems you may never be able to solve. The same with your children—reward in public, correct in private.

Make it clear to your wife that if she is the one with the tendency to second-guess you, not to do it publicly. Women often try to keep their husbands from making bad decisions, but when it is done in front of others it merely undermines his authority. When a wife works with her husband and second-guesses his decisions, he loses face in the eyes of others. Either one second-guessing the other creates in the children and any employees a failure to trust in decisions.

**Number Twenty-Three:** *If spouses travel, they want to be conquering heroes when they come home.*

A friend's wife joked that when her husband conquers the battle of the marketplace, coming home and giving her the paycheck makes her "more than a conqueror."

Humorous as it sounds, either spouse coming off the road deserves a warrior's welcome. Facing temptations outside the home, overcoming them in the power of the Holy Spirit, and returning with love and grace in the heart for the family really makes us overcomers. Homecoming is always a celebratory occasion.

**Number Twenty-Four:** *Work with what you have to get what you want.*

You didn't marry perfection, just potential. What your marriage becomes is what you put into the potential to develop it. The quality of your investment will determine the value of the product. Marriage is the product of the quality of character each invests in the other. Don't bemoan the fact that you don't have what you think you need to get what you want. You work with what you have, not what you don't have, not what you hope to have. Mediocre men complain about not having what they need to get started, whether in marriage or in business. You never have enough to get started—you just start.

My son Paul started marriage with a love seat and a chair in a garage apartment (no bed), and driving a worn-out Corvair with only two gears (no reverse) and a Volkswagen van. Twenty-five years later, he has a wonderful wife, three exemplary children, a beautiful home, and a powerful ministry and testimony.

The end result is what counts, not how you start. "Despise not the day of small beginnings."[12]

**Number Twenty-Five:** *Discipline yourself before you try to discipline others.*

Discipline is not based on hatred but on preference. You don't discipline yourself because you hate yourself, but because you love yourself. You don't lose weight because you hate being fat, you lose weight because you prefer being thin. Whatever you prefer in life determines your self-discipline. If you prefer parties to having a steady job and good relationship, then you will be disciplined in preparing for and going to parties, but you won't be disciplined on the job or in the home. If you prefer a peaceful home to having raucous friends, then you will discipline yourself to creating peace at home while shunning friends that disturb it.

Controlling your appetite is more than gastronomic. It is your thoughts, passions, and habits. You cannot expect discipline of your children to succeed when they see you fail in it. Before you're tempted to discourage your spouse or child, think of the example you set and determine to change yourself before starting in on them.

**Number Twenty-Six:** *You cannot correct in others what is wrong in your own life.*

The characteristics of the kingdom emanate from the character of the king. In other words, whatever is in the character of the king will become the characteristics in the kingdom. True of the Kingdom of God. True of a home.

In a home, you represent the king and your family is the kingdom. When your character is negative, so are the characteristics of those in the home. To punish your children for what you see wrong in their lives is an error if it is also a characteristic of your life.

Change must come from the top voluntarily by revelation, or it will come from the bottom by revolution.

Discipline yourself first, then others. You cannot correct in others what is wrong in your own life.

**Number Twenty-Seven:** *You're a poor specimen if you cannot stand the pressure of adversity.*[13]

Strength is tested by resistance to pressure. In weight training, resistance to pressure tones and strengthens a body. As we grow in our manhood, resistance to pressure tones and strengthens our character. Resistance to pressure strengthens our friendships, enables us to graduate from school, stay on a job, and build a career.

A marriage shows its strength when it is under pressures that could pull it apart. Resisting the pressures of employment difficulties, disease, or even a misunderstanding among relatives will reveal the strength you have built into the marriage. Standing the test and remaining united is a strong statement to yourselves as well as the world around you.

The only constant in maturity is change. It is difficult to live with change, but impossible to live without it. Change is a constant process in growth and maturity. Change always comes by way of crisis. Since change is normal to life, crisis is normal as well. Your ability to handle change and crisis shows your level of maturity as a man.

A tidy, gray-haired woman sat next to me on an airplane and after discovering I was a minister, poured her heart out. She was going through a divorce. Didn't want it. Tried to avoid it. Pled with her husband. Dealt with the issues, but could not deal with him. He was a churchgoer. Usher. Sunday School teacher. But he was adamant in his ways and would not consider any change in his life or their marriage. He took her for granted, was a poor steward of her love, indifferent to her needs or desires, and would not accept any responsibility for their troubles. In his mind, it was her problem and that was it. She had changed, he hadn't, and it was her fault.

Why was she divorcing him? BOREDOM! She had gone back to school, graduated, went to work, achieved success, and wanted to experience more than the ordinary, second rate, common, take-it-for-granted-and-leave-it-alone lifestyle. She wanted to do something interesting, take up new hobbies, watch the sun set on a dozen different horizons. He would not listen to her. Did not want to hear about her accomplishments. Refused to treat her as a person with real needs, appetites, and desires. These aren't scriptural grounds for divorce, yet they are physical grounds for great unhappiness.

**Number Twenty-Eight:** *Ladies, minister to your husband sexually—it's your strength.*

This is for your wife to read. When a man has been ministered to sexually, it's easy to share his heart. Women want to share their hearts first, but for men it's generally the other way around. I once had a woman on a radio call-in show tell me she couldn't get her husband to talk. I asked her when the last time was that she had ministered to him sexually. She said, "two months." I said, "tonight's the night." Later that evening I was preparing for a meeting at a local church when an usher barged into the little dressing room I was in and shook my hand, beaming from ear to ear. "That was my wife on the radio today," he said. "Did you share your heart with her?" "Yessir," he answered, then abruptly turned and walked away!

**Number Twenty-Nine:** *Don't try to make your spouse into the image you had of what you wanted to marry.*

What you had was a fantasy, what you have is reality. Often women, more than men, treat the wedding as a "start construction" agreement. Wrong. You're starting a life together, with all the bumps and bruises it brings—not starting a method whereby you will change each other into your ideal.

*Number Thirty:* *Communicate. Communicate. Communicate.*

A TV host once interviewed me about a renewal of marriage vows which I had performed publicly one Valentines Day. "There is a four-letter word for intercourse," I told him. He nervously glanced around, but kept the mike to my face. "It's T-A-L-K!"

"Come now, and let us reason together, saith the LORD."[14] Reason is the capacity for knowing the truth. Unless you are willing to listen to reason, you will never discover truth. Reasoning judges evidence, credibility and believability to learn truth. Reason organizes facts upon which to make a decision, and does not allow feelings to dictate decisions. The irresistible husband is a reasonable man. He listens.

Listening is the first art of communication. Listening to his wife gives her value. He shows respect for his family's opinions, ideas, and desires. Self-respect is more valuable than self-esteem.

A poor salesman always talks past the point of the sale. A poor husband interrupts before his wife is finished talking. A poor parent frustrates a child by not offering time to listen to him. Real men know that time invested in listening is rewarded by relationships that make life worth living.

"The more you speak, the less your words mean."[15] The most explosive force on earth comes from the smallest bit of matter. The more concise and cogent we make our statements, the more impact they have. The more we speak, the more we diffuse the import of our words. When we learn to sow seeds of truth, God can make them grow in the mind and heart where they are sown. Teaching your children how to speak, from teaching them how to listen, gives them power in communication.

"An unreliable messenger can cause a lot of trouble. Reliable communication permits progress."[16] Relationship is based on communication. We most often see a communication gap between parents and children, not a generation gap. If you don't communicate you can't relate.

In return for implementing this Guide to Daily Living, the irresistible husband receives respect, affection, attention, and honor.

[1] Proverbs 4:7
[2] Proverbs 3:13-16
[3] Proverbs 8:11
[4] James 1:5
[5] 1 Corinthians 1:30
[6] Romans 10:17
[7] Genesis 17:5
[8] I Timothy 3:4
[9] Deuteronomy 25:4
[10] Matthew 10:10
[11] Psalm 133:1 TLB
[12] Zechariah 4:10
[13] Proverbs 24:10
[14] Isaiah 1:18
[15] Ecclesiastes 6:11
[16] Proverbs 13:17 TLB

# CHAPTER ELEVEN

# EARN A GOOD LIVING

When God made male and female He gave us each our strengths and uniquenesses. Before God created Eve He gave Adam a job. It's still the same pattern today. No job—no wife.

We have no idea how long Adam was productive at work before Eve came along, but it must have been some time because Adam had already named all the animals. God made Adam a steward of the earth and gave him the responsibility to guide, guard and govern God's creation on earth. Adam was satisfied with his stewardship and fulfilled in its productivity.

"And God said, Let the earth bring forth grass, the herb yielding seed, and the fruit tree yielding fruit after his kind, whose seed is in itself, upon the earth: and it was so."[1] Each seed-bearing plant or creature had to plant its seed for the process of reproduction. Adam took pleasure in overseeing that production.

For man to be reproduced on the earth, Adam needed to plant his seed. The place of planting was in the woman. Eve was Adam's "completer" and fulfilled the reproductive process of childbirth. Though Adam had the power of the job and money, Eve had the power of sex.

Adam was fulfilled in the reproduction process both in his job and in his relationship with Eve. God made the reproduction process both at work and with Eve not only satisfying but fulfilling. To this day, men are basically satisfied in participating in this reproductive process at work and home, which is why I only half joke when I say that most men are happy with a paycheck and sex, and don't notice much else. Paycheck and sex. Happiness.

But how do you ensure that paycheck?

## YOUR GIFT

God's Word instructs us that "a man's gift makes room for him."[2]

Remember Gene whose gift of grace made room for him in Patti's heart. Consider the man who tried unsuccessfully for months to get a date with a young lady he admired and wanted to meet. Failure followed failure. Finally one day he sent her flowers, and a date was quickly agreed. His gift made room for him. Or the husband whose wife was against his buying a new car. But once he gave her the vacation she wanted with the family, she told him to get the new car. His gift made room for him. Or the man who bribed the judge and his charge was dismissed. Sordid, but his gift made room for him.

The Bible tells of Barnabas, a new convert to Christ who sold land, then brought the profits and laid them at the apostles' feet. God called him a "good man, full of the Holy Ghost and faith."[3] Later we read of him ministering with the apostles, and then traveling and ministering as the companion of Paul the Apostle.[4] His gift made room for him with the very people to whom he gave it.

I have friends who minister and travel with me around the world, some of whom have been with me for years. They are my dearest and most trustworthy friends. Our relationship began when they became partners with me in sharing the Gospel with the men of this world. Their gift made room for them. First they gave of their time, in attending the meetings we held. Then they gave treasure as they supported the ministry financially. And finally they gave of their talent as they began to minister with me.

It all began with one gift.

Every man has a gift he can give. It will make room for him.

Like the young man trying to get a date, however, sometimes the first attempt to use our gift will fail. The willingness to be responsible for success is based on the willingness to be responsible for failure. Coach John Wooden's teams won ten championships based on this one truth: "Failure to prepare is preparation for failure." Lack of preparation is the number one cause of business failure. But failure is not the worst thing in the world—quitting is. Being willing to fail, preparing your gift, one day it will make room for you, and when that happens, it will fulfill you beyond your own imaginations.[5]

## JOSEPH'S GIFT

Joseph was a young man who was sold down the river by his brothers, then bought by a man named Potiphar. Joseph became Potiphar's trusted steward, but was jailed on false accusations by Potiphar's vain and arrogant wife who had the "spirit of the spoiler." While in jail, Joseph was again raised to the highest trusteeship. He interpreted a dream of a butler who promised to remember him when he was released from prison, but failed to do so.

A year later, when Pharaoh had a dream and none of his magicians could interpret it, the butler remembered his fault and told Pharaoh of Joseph's gift to interpret dreams—a gift from God. When Joseph told Pharaoh the meaning of his dream, Pharaoh realized that no other in his whole kingdom had such wisdom, and he elevated Joseph to be Prime Minister of his domain. It was the Holy Spirit's gift of interpreting dreams operating in the life of Joseph that brought him to the attention of Pharaoh—and to the highest position in the land.[6] His gift, a gloriously spiritual gift from God, made room for him.

Whether physical, financial, or spiritual, all gifts make room for the giver where and when they are counted.

Rahab is listed in the lineage of Jesus. Her gift made room for her there. Though classed as a harlot, it was the grace in her heart that hid God's servants, spared their lives, and resulted in her being spared when the city was demolished.

Nancy and I celebrated fifty-four years of marriage the year she died. It was Nancy's gift of forgiveness that kept us married. Her gift made so much room for her in my heart and life that I could never thank her enough for staying married to me all those years.

*Your gift will make room for you as well.* Diligence has its own reward, and exercising your gift diligently compounds the rewards.

## GEORGE'S GIFT

My friend George, who took me to that delicious steak dinner, told me another story that night. He had left his mother's household, where they were tossed from housing project to housing project, and he sought out his biological father who took him in. The father tried to do right by him and taught him his trade in construction as well as taking him to church. In a conversation one Sunday, his father said, "George, always be the first one on the job, and always be the last to leave, and no matter what happens, even if your job depends on it, never, ever tell a lie. If you've made a mistake, own up to it and admit it right away. Never try to lie your way out of anything."

Armed with that bit of wisdom, when George finished the military he married his bride Norma and struck out to ply his trade. Weather kept construction workers from making a great deal of money in George's hometown, but he plugged away doing his best, becoming involved in church, even accepting the unpaid position of youth pastor. When a large construction firm came to town to create a housing development, they asked George's father to be their project manager. George's father felt he was too old at that time to start something requiring so much energy, so he urged them instead to interview George.

George got the job and instantly his gift was put to the test. One of the senior partners in the enormous firm came to him the first day and said, "this row of five homes needs to be completed in a week for the families to move in." George looked down the row of houses and saw homes with foundations and framing, but little else. Distraught, he encouraged himself by realizing this man had been in the business much longer than George had, and if he said the houses had to be completed in a week, there must be a way to do it. George simply needed to learn what this man had already discovered.

"I'll be gone all week," he told Norma by telephone the afternoon of his very first day. "This project is going to require a lot of work."

Then he prayed, and mapped out a schedule for his subcontractors to work 'round the clock.

A month later the senior partner returned to check on George's project. He casually asked George whatever happened to those five houses.

"We moved the families in right on time," George answered.

The partner's jaw went slack, but he covered his embarrassment and looked over the schedule George had kept to move in the families. The next week, the partner called George and said he was sending three new project managers out for George to train them.

"But I don't know the job myself yet," George remonstrated. "How can I possibly train someone else?"

"Just tell them what you know," the partner said. "We'll give you a bonus."

George trained the three men, who turned out to be good solid men who stayed with the company for years. George received a bonus, then a promotion to train all the project managers in the entire company. For three years every time George talked with one of the partners, it was to receive the offer of a bonus, a raise, a promotion, or all three. Then they seemed to change.

"Come meet us for coffee," the senior partner said seriously over the telephone.

George met them at the restaurant they designated, feeling happy since it usually meant more money for his family. But this time they took him to the back of the restaurant to a darkened table, ordered coffee for him, and started asking tough questions. George became increasingly uncomfortable as the questions became more personal and he felt his margin for answering incorrectly increased.

"We need to know something else," one of the two senior partners said. "If there was something wrong, something that one of us was responsible for, not just a company problem, but something serious that you know is linked to one of us. If that were the case, would you lie for us?"

The next few moments felt like hours as George quickly pondered the question and its ramifications. He knew these men and trusted them. Neither of them would do something wrong unless they had simply made a mistake. Why not cover for them? These men trusted him, had been generous with him, and he trusted them. Why not lie for them? But his father's admonition came ringing into his ears, "no matter what happens, even if your job depends on it, never, ever tell a lie." George knew the answer he would have to give. He quickly thought through how he would tell Norma he had lost his job, and made a brief plan in his mind of how to find work with another firm. Then he took a deep breath and gave his answer.

"No sir," George said, "even if it was for one of you, as much as I respect both of you, I could not lie for you."

Fear raced through George's heart and his hands became sweaty. The senior partners asked another couple of questions and George answered them numbly, waiting for the blow to fall.

"George, about lying for us," one of the men finally started. "If you had said yes, you would have worked with us for a long time. You work well, manage well, and we would always have kept you employed."

George's mind leaped back to the words he would choose to soften the blow for Norma, and raced forward to the firms where he could apply the next morning.

"But since you answered that you wouldn't lie for us," the senior partner droned on, "we can now make you an offer that we could never make to a man who is willing to lie. We'd like to bring you on as a junior partner!"

George's gift made room for him, and as he relied on what he knew was right, truth became his salvation. He was promoted beyond his wildest dreams to the position he still holds today, twenty years later.

## LYING WILL ALWAYS SABOTAGE YOU

To lie is to act like, and put yourself in agreement with, the devil. Satan is the "father of lies."[7] God said clearly, "Thou shalt not lie!" To tell the truth is to act like, and put yourself in agreement with, Jesus Christ. Jesus IS the Truth.[8]

Twelve Israelite men were sent into Canaan to spy out the land. Ten brought back an evil report, saying it was impossible for the Israelites to move into Canaan, and basically slandered the Word of God by calling God a liar. Their punishment was death, along with the entire generation that believed their bad report.

You cannot trust in a lie or liars, or someone who calls God a liar by not believing Him.

A real man loves truth, shuns lying, and believes God. He does not adapt to the world's culture of cheating, lying, stealing, immorality, and putting himself before others.

*Telling the truth might be one of the hardest things you can do in life, but once done, it certainly is the most exhilarating.* The enlargement of spirit, freedom from guilt, and absence of the torment of mind is well worth the price of truth-telling. "Truth stands the test of time; lies are soon exposed."[9] When lies are exposed, everyone suffers.

Living with a lie is only exceeded by living with a liar. Pity the woman whose plight is to live with a man whom she knows is a liar. All adulterers, addicts and abusers are liars because they are all in denial, lying to themselves.

A woman wants a man of good and godly character. Christlike character is what she can commit to wholeheartedly, yield herself to and depend upon entirely.

"Lord, who may go and find refuge and shelter in your tabernacle up on your holy hill? Anyone who leads a blameless life and is truly sincere. Anyone who refuses to slander others, does not listen to gossip, never harms his neighbor, speaks out against sin, criticizes those committing it, commends the faithful followers of the Lord, keeps a promise even if it ruins him, does not crush his debtors with high interest rates, and refuses to testify against the innocent despite the bribes offered him—such a man shall stand firm forever.[10]

Those are the characteristics and qualifications of a true man of character according to God's Word. A trustworthy man.

## TRUTH IS YOUR ROCK

Truth is the rock upon which we build right character. Jesus Christ *is* Truth. Jesus said, "I am the way, the truth, and the life."[11] From within, out of the heart spring issues of life, so the Spirit of Truth must occupy the very core of our being. Christ's Spirit is the Spirit of Truth!

God cannot lie. "God is not a man that he should lie ...." The truth is always right, and a lie is always wrong. Any untruth is immoral on personal grounds, and illegitimate for social reasons. There is nothing trustworthy, stable, and good in a man that practices lies.

No lie can serve the purposes of God. Jesus taught us that the devil is a "murderer" because he is the progenitor of lies, and lies murder the truth. Satan has always regarded a lie as entirely legitimate, and sees no reason whatever why men should not lie when they consider it necessary. What is morally wrong, inconsistent with the character of God, and destructive of morality and society cannot be made to be right even if its purpose is to save a life.

The devil believed that a man would sacrifice anything for the sake of his life. That was the basis for his temptation of Jesus. He tempted the young student, Cassie, at the Columbine school shooting in the same way, thinking she would lie about God to spare her own life. She would not, and told the gunman pointing at her that she believed in God. Had she lied and denied God, what proof could she have had that he wouldn't have killed her anyway, and those would have been her last words on this earth? She went to be with Jesus immediately, with the testimony of her belief in Him ringing as her last words. How can we do less than this heroic school girl, to stand for truth, regardless of what is at stake?

The prophet Isaiah deplored the profusion of lying in his country when he prophesied, "For our transgressions are mul-

tiplied before thee, and our sins testify against us: for our transgressions are with us; and as for our iniquities, we know them;
In transgressing and lying against the LORD, and departing
away from our God, speaking oppression and revolt, conceiv-
ing and uttering from the heart words of falsehood. And judgment is turned away backward, and justice standeth afar off:
for truth is fallen in the street, and equity cannot enter."[12]

When truth fell in Isaiah's streets, morality had nothing
to stand upon, and its collapse was a disaster socially, eco-
nomically and spiritually, individually and corporately. Our
culture today is no different.

The "Irresistible Husband" is willing to separate himself from
his culture, and commit to the culture of Christianity. Even to
the extent that he will lay down his life for the One who paid
the price for him on the Cross, and for the ones entrusted to his
care—his family. Holding to truth, working hard, preparing
your gift and believing God that it will make room for you—
these are the attributes of working men who really win.

To be the "Irresistible Husband" is the desire of most men,
the dream of every wife, and part of the purpose of God's
redemptive plan for your life.

[1]  Genesis 1:11
[2]  Proverbs 18:16
[3]  Acts 11:24
[4]  Acts 4:32; 11:24; 13:2
[5]  Proverbs 18:16
[6]  Genesis 40-41
[7]  John 8:44 NIV
[8]  John 14:6
[9]  Proverbs 12:19 TLB
[10]  Psalm 15:1-5 TLB
[11]  John 14:6
[12]  Isaiah 59:12-14

# CHAPTER TWELVE

# KEEP YOUR WIFE IN LOVE WITH YOU

You may have heard about the hospitalized man whose wife asked the doctor privately for the prognosis. "He just needs home-cooked meals every day, no arguments, and sex three times a week, then he'll be fine," the doctor told her. When she returned to the hospital room, the husband eagerly asked, "What did the doctor say?"

"You're going to die," she answered.

All men laugh at that joke. We know our wives don't want to cater to us, and perhaps we even begrudge them or blame them for it. But what can we do to become the kind of man she adores and loves to help? We know we want the paycheck and sex, and we just talked about how to keep a paycheck, now what about the other part?

## LEARN TO LOVE

Jesus said, "Love your neighbor as yourself." For God to have commanded us to do something outside our ability would have been grossly unfair. He commanded love, which means love must be a choice, an act of our will, not an accident that happens when we least expect it.

God commands us in His "Ten Commandments" first and foremost to love Him with all our heart, mind, soul and body. "But if any man love God, the same is known of him."[1] When a man loves God, his love for God is known to all because our hearts are right toward others. The desires of our hearts do not hurt, wound, or cause pain and loss to others when

131

we love God first. God is love, therefore anyone who is developing in the character of Christ in God is filled with the love of God. The love of God is being shed abroad in his heart by the Holy Spirit.[2]

God's last commandment of the ten is, "Don't covet," which means, "don't desire dishonest gain, or always be grasping to have more." In some translations the word is translated "greed" which is a form of lust. It is the opposite of "being content with what you have."[3] Covetousness is idolatrous in nature because it is a form of loving the world at the expense of remembering God.[4] To get from A to Z, from the first commandment through to the last, requires that we love God first.

The most powerful motives in human life are hate, fear and greed. However one is more powerful than all three of them and that is LOVE. God *is* love! Love overcomes obstacles, triumphs over evil, and knows no end.

The way we drop one thing to grab another is a principle I call "the expulsive power of a new affection." A girl who loves stuffed animals discovers boys one day and suddenly, in the expulsive power of the new affection, out go the toys as she goes in search of the boys. A boy loves to build models of airplanes and cars until he discovers girls built like magazine models, and in the expulsive power of the new affection, he exchanges one for the other. In dealing with greed and covetousness lodged in your heart, you won't get rid of it by berating yourself, but by becoming filled with love for God and others. The new affection, thinking of your wife and family first, will dislodge and expel the old, thinking only of self. It won't "just happen," because *love is a choice.*

People tend to love those who love them. To ensure your wife will love you forever, learn to love her, then practice it forever. The "Golden Rule" Jesus gave in His "Sermon on the Mount" is, "Do for others what you want them to do for you. This is the teaching of the laws of Moses in a nutshell."[5]

## EIGHT TRUTHS CONCERNING LOVE

Understand and thoroughly embrace the following truths about love. They are simple, cogent, potent, and can serve you throughout life.

### 1. LOVE'S DESIRE - *Love desires to benefit others even at the expense of self because love desires to give.*

"For God so loved the world, that he gave his only begotten Son, that whosoever believeth in him should not perish, but have everlasting life."[6] God so loved the world that He gave Jesus Christ even at the expense of Himself because He wanted to give salvation to men. Love's desire is a passion and an obedience to do what is necessary for the one loved.

In the Old Testament story of Jacob, he gave seven years of his life for Rachel, then another seven. The Bible says of him, "And Jacob served seven years for Rachel; and they seemed unto him but a few days, for the love he had for her."[7] Jacob's years of service seemed like a small price because of the great love he had.

### 2. LOVE'S EVIDENCE - *Obedience is the evidence of love.*

"If a man love me, he will keep my words: and my Father will love him, and we will come unto him, and make our abode with him."[8] Obedience is the evidence of love and manifestation is based on obedience. God doesn't manifest Himself to us because we love Him but rather because we obey Him.

This was Saul's great lesson when he disobeyed God and lost the kingdom. "And Samuel said, Hath the LORD as great delight in burnt offerings and sacrifices, as in obeying the voice of the LORD? Behold, to obey is better than sacrifice, and to hearken than the fat of rams."[9]

## 3. LOVE'S DEPTH - *You know the depth of loving by the degree of giving.*

"Greater love hath no man than this, that a man lay down his life for his friends."[10]

You can give without loving, but you cannot love without giving. The nature of love is found in the quality of giving. You know the nature of God's love by His gift to us—Jesus. The depth of love is shown in the degree of our giving of self for others. I knew the depth of my wife Nancy's love for me by how much of herself she gave me. For her, it was total with a capital "T."

## 4. LOVE'S AMOUNT – *Realizing how much we have been forgiven determines how much we love.*

"And when they had nothing to pay, he frankly forgave them both. Tell me therefore, which of them will love him most?"[11]

Andy left Katy for a woman he met in an Internet chat room. He spent months with her, while still working with his wife. Katy died daily to herself, sought God with her entire being just to continue living, and learned to love God as she never had before. Katy and some prayer partners held on to Andy in prayer. Even though she was emotionally drained, and had no feeling for Andy, she continued to pray for him out of obedience to her commitment to God when she recited her vows to Andy.

One Saturday morning at work she needed some information and called Andy for it. He was in bed with his mistress' head on his arm. He cradled the phone with one hand, while caressing the woman with the other. As Katy prepared to end the conversation, she suddenly spoke to Andy in a voice and with a spirit she did not know she possessed. She did something that could only be by inspiration of the Holy Spirit.

"Andy, I love you," she said.

He dropped the woman's head and rolled over on his side, hesitating a moment before saying, "I love you too, Katy."

When his lover heard those words, she jumped out of bed, dressed, and stormed out of the room. He never saw her again.

With great repentance and sorrow, Andy earnestly sought God. After several weeks he began to pray with Katy, and a few months later they were reconciled and renewed their vows afresh. Today as they share their testimony, she tells of the incredible work of God's grace in her heart that enabled her to forgive him, and he tells of the amazing abundance of gratitude and love he has for her.

Andy was resistible in sin, but became irresistible through genuine sorrow of repentance and love's desire for Katy. How much have you been forgiven? Does your wife forgive you every day for your various shortcomings? Every day God has to forgive you for all your sins—both known and unknown by you. Understanding that enlarges your capacity to love.

*5. LOVE'S QUALIFICATION - Love is the qualification for speaking the truth.*

"But speaking the truth in love, may grow up into him in all things ...." [12]

Affection guarantees reception. Trying to minister a word of truth to your wife, or family, or anyone, without the love of God has little truth worth hearing. Not every word spoken to us has the right to be heard. Not everything people say is necessary for us to hear. What is not spoken in love can do us harm rather than good.

"Howbeit when He, the Spirit of truth, is come, He will guide you into all truth." [13] "Sanctify them through thy truth: thy word is truth. [14]

*6. LOVE'S GREATNESS – Love conquers all.*

"And now abide faith, hope, love, these three; but the greatest of these is love." [15] Faith and hope will end, but love never will—which makes love the greatest. What faith has obtained, and hope has realized, love will carry on. God is love.

### 7. LOVE'S BALANCE – *Those who love God hate evil.*

"Ye that love the LORD, hate evil."[16] God has a divine love of right and divine scorn of wrong. At His disposal is "the wine press of the fierceness of the wrath of almighty God."[17] Love has boundaries—lust knows no limits. Love has balance—lust is one-sided. Christianity inspires hatred of sin. Love involves hatred. To support the principle of good necessitates antagonism toward the perversion of evil.

The writer of Hebrews spoke of Jesus by quoting from Psalms, "Thou hast loved righteousness and hated iniquity."[18] Christianity does not suppress feelings of love and hatred. Christianity intensifies them! Today many are unbalanced in their Christ life. They are so caught up with trying to love God they have forgotten to hate sin. "For your obedience is come abroad unto all men. I am glad therefore on your behalf: but yet I would have you wise unto that which is good, and simple concerning evil."[19]

Last Sunday while sitting in my office I was scrolling down my rolodex on my cell phone when I came across the number of an old friend who had served in the ministry. I dialed the number and his wife answered. In the first few sentences she told me they had been divorced for several months—after more than three decades of marriage. She would not divulge the reason, but when I finished the conversation I had an assumption that Internet porn had entrapped him. A few minutes later I was standing on my feet shouting until the walls reverberated with my hatred of Satan and sin that so easily besets men. In every way possible I gave vent to the furious hatred I had for evil. I'm glad no one was around to hear me, but I am not ashamed of my heat and fire.

Christianity not only inspires hatred of sin but also restrains hatred by forbidding anger because of personal dislike or selfishness or offense, and by fixing our hatred on principles, not persons. The Christian character needs wrath for its own protection. The very love of the highest demands its scorn of the lowest. "I hate and abhor lying, but thy law do I love."[20] Christianity is the greatest love-producing power in the world because it is also the greatest fountain of godly wrath.

*Love desires that which benefits the one loved, but hates that which hurts what we love.*

"These six things doth the LORD hate: yea, seven are an abomination unto him: A proud look, a lying tongue, and hands that shed innocent blood, An heart that deviseth wicked imaginations, feet that be swift in running to mischief, A false witness that speaketh lies, and he that soweth discord among brethren."[21]

"The fear of the LORD is to hate evil: pride, and arrogancy, and the evil way, and the froward mouth, do I hate."[22]

"Hate the evil, and love the good, and establish judgment in the gate: it may be that the LORD God of hosts will be gracious unto the remnant of Joseph."[23]

There is no question that contemporary ministry is so saturated with the promotion of the love of God that they omit the balance which is a hatred for evil. Personally, I am convinced the reason for many of the ills we face in our churches is an unbalanced condition where Christians who love God do not hate what God hates. "I hate divorce."[24] If we won't hate what God hates, and agree with His Word, our Christianity is as good as sleeping on a mattress that's placed on a pile of dung.

## 8. LOVE'S MATURITY – *Covenant men put away childish things.*

"When I was a child, I spake as a child, I understood as a child, I thought as a child: but when I became a man, I put away childish things."[25]

You can be a male, a man or a covenant man. We talk about being an irresistible husband to your wife. Great. But what kind of a man are you to God? Fully mature men are covenant men. That's your lesson for the next chapter, and the biggest test for your love yet.

How have you fared so far? Have you attained to that stature of the measure of Christ that makes you a true gentleman, one who is respected and admired by his own family, who can be trusted, and who is worthy of commitment? When God says he hates divorce do you believe Him? Enough to hate it, too? "We only believe what we obey," a great friend once said.

What do you think about your wife? What you think about her will determine your relationship with her, and develop the character of your marriage. What kind of a man are you becoming today?

[1] I Corinthians 8:3
[2] Romans 5:5
[3] Hebrews 13:5
[4] Colossians 3:5 [Unger's Bible Dictionary]
[5] Matthew 7:12 TLB
[6] John 3:16
[7] Genesis 29:20
[8] John 14:23
[9] I Samuel 15:22
[10] John 15:13
[11] Luke 7:42
[12] Ephesians 4:15
[13] John 16:13
[14] John 17:17
[15] I Corinthians 13:13
[16] Psalm 97:10
[17] Revelation 19:15
[18] Psalm 45:7; Hebrew 1:9
[19] Romans 16:19
[20] Psalm 119:163
[21] Proverbs 6:16-19
[22] Proverbs 8:13
[23] Amos 5:15
[24] Malachi 2:16
[25] I Corinthians 13:11

# CHAPTER THIRTEEN

# BE A COVENANT MAN!

To be a Covenant Man is to accept in full, and to fulfill, the terms of the Covenant given to us by Christ, to the best of our ability. To aspire to be known not merely as a man, but as a Christlike man.

Jesus gave us the New Covenant, based on His work on the Cross. By doing so, He set an absolute standard for un-selfishness. He was its standard.[1] Jesus presented to you His kingdom with its service to God and man, that was to be above home, friends, comfort, life.[2] He made no room for exemptions, excuses, or exceptions.

Jesus also set the standard for absolute purity. He toler-ated no uncleanness whatsoever. His example was that the inner heart and its imagery and desire must be pure.[3] Outer or inner sin—from hand or from eye—must be gone.[4]

And He set an absolute standard of love.[5] Neither dirt, nor poverty, nor social inferiority were amendments to the "Law of Love."[6] Jesus set the standard when He loved to the limit of life.[7] His "law of love" makes it impossible not to love.

Jesus Himself was the standard He set. He was unchange-able. He had been before Abraham.[8] He would be forever.[9] The absolute teacher was the absolute lesson.

*Your generation needs Truth above all else.* There is no other basis upon which to build character and a society that is good, godly, moral and sound. Jesus is Truth. Jesus is God's Word in human form. The worst experience in my life is to read the Word and have it seem dead. Nothing is more awful to the human soul than to be dead to Truth. Nothing is more fulfilling than to have Truth spring up within me, coming to my remembrance, filling my mind, my heart—my very gut! —in inspired revelation. Thrilling!

God is not partial. No one can be denied Truth when they seek it. Likewise, no one is exempt from any part of Scripture. We cannot receive only the Truth that appeals to us, which is why Truth is something only a Covenant Man can take. The wishy-washy, flaky, and wannabe's will sell out and give up when confronted with hard Truth. But a Covenant Man is a man who embraces even the most difficult truths of Scripture. He is one on whom a woman, a family, a whole culture can depend—and a man on whom God does depend.

The Lord told us to love a wife even as Christ loves the Church.[10] A Covenant Man reads that and believes it is possible for him to do it. He accepts the challenge as the standard by which he will measure himself, as a lifestyle to which he can aspire, as a Truth upon which he will build his indestructible marriage.

How does a Covenant Man love his wife? The same way Christ loves the Church.

My friend Jim had matured into manhood, yet not completely become a Covenant Man, when he faced the worst situation he could ever imagine, one in which I hope you will never find yourself.

## You Have A Choice

"You have a choice. Love her or leave her."

Those words pierced his heart and I saw him wince as he heard them. He had come to me because he discovered the greatest horror he could imagine—his wife was having an affair. He wanted an answer but instead he got a choice. Jim had to face that choice because he had been running from it, and it had only compounded his hurt and confusion.

"I love her but I'm not sure how much," he said in a low, slow hesitant voice. "I'd have to set conditions if we stayed together."

"The truth is, you can't love her enough no matter how hard you try," I said. "You need God's love to forgive her, the same love with which He forgave you—unconditional love. You can only have it by the Spirit of God Who sheds love abroad in your heart."[11]

With those words, he began to cry. The struggle was tremendous. Could he love her unconditionally? Forgive her completely?

We live in a conditional world. The conditions of the weather tell us what kind of day or opportunities we will have, or what kind of crop or animal we can raise. Conditions in contracts limit us. Work and living conditions build us up or bring us down.

*The condition of man's nature makes him incapable of loving as God loves.* Man's nature is flawed, and the love God endowed him with at creation has been misshapen by sin. The best man can do with his flawed nature is to manifest a simulation of God's love, which often seems impossible because of "conditions." This is why the world is starved for love, and cannot be satisfied with mere human love which is imperfect, impaired and has been perverted to lust. We see signs and evidences of love in a natural setting, but God's true love is supernatural.

God's love died in the heart of man when he died to the relationship with God the Father. God's love was shown to men, but little shown from men to God. Obedience is the evidence of love, and we have seen little of it. It took the advent of Christ on earth to reveal the full measure of God's unconditional love. *"Having loved his own, he loved them to the end."*[12] Christ loved men even when they called for

His crucifixion. He was and is the end-all for men, proving it in a most inglorious manner at death.

Such love as God's is absent from the human heart and must be imparted when a new heart is given through the covenant with Christ. God promises, "A new heart also will I give you, and a new spirit will I put within you: and I will take away the stony heart out of your flesh, and I will give you an heart of flesh."[13] *With God's Spirit at work within our new heart, we can actually begin to love as God loves.*

Jim struggled in a fight to the death—death of himself, which would allow him to become alive in Christ in a way he'd never been. Could he embrace his wife and fight for the marriage? Could he ever trust her again? Jim had to die to himself, his fleshly nature, and seek God to fill his heart with the God-kind of love. He made the decision, then spent months walking it out. Years have passed since our meeting that day and today Jim cannot thank God enough. "It was worth every hour and minute," he says of the ordeal. Through it, he not only resurrected his marriage, but he became a Covenant Man.

Jim's story reminds me of Jacob, who spent fourteen years laboring for the hand of Rachel in marriage, and after marrying, said it seemed "but a few days" because of the great love he had for her.

*Love depends on giving, and giving forgiveness and grace is the greatest gift we can give.* To the extent we realize how much we ourselves have been forgiven, we can grow in unconditional love for others.

A male cannot love right because he is an immature man, still childish, manifesting the characteristics of a child rather then those of a mature man. A man accepts responsibility for his actions, even those of his family and the world in which he lives and works, but he can't love right because he has never become man enough to admit God is always right and he is often wrong. He cannot admit his need of something more, something outside himself, to complete His manhood.

A covenant man understands that his morality, goodness, and achievements are not sufficient qualities for acceptance in God's kingdom. Through repentance and faith in Christ, every day he experiences God's forgiveness and grace and is truly a "new creation in Christ Jesus." The truest Christian is the finest gentleman. Only the genuine covenant man, gentleman as he is, can become an irresistible husband.

Look at how each—male, man and covenant man—regards his wife, using the standard Christ set, that a man must love his wife as Christ loves the Church.

## THREE CHARACTERISTICS OF CHRIST'S LOVE

### 1. Christ loves the Church *unconditionally*.

God's love is unconditional. His promises are conditional. He loves us enough to forgive us, whatever our sin. When a male "loves" a woman he wants her for his benefit, which is lust, not love. He wants what she can give him, whether its sex or her steady paycheck or her willingness to put up with him.

The man loves his wife, but he loves her conditionally, when she serves or pleases him. He loves her when she's thin, or in a good mood, or when she cooks for him. He loves her for what she does, not for who she is. He's a man, but still has childish traits.

A covenant man loves his wife unconditionally. He loves her for who she is, regardless. He gives himself to her in love, with concern for her welfare more than for his. As Jim learned, a covenant man's love is made unconditional by the love of God shed abroad in his heart by the Holy Spirit.

## 2. *Christ loves us **sacrificially**.*

The male makes no sacrifice for his wife. He wants it all and takes it from her. He lets her make all the sacrifices while he makes none, and generally without gratitude or appreciation toward her. Selfish and self-centered, he is a taker rather than a giver.

The man will make some minimal sacrifices, but it's "play by my rules or I'm not going to play." In his immaturity, he doesn't understand what it is to give of himself sacrificially.

But for the covenant man, nothing is too good for her. He loves her with God's abundant love, and his grace is without limit. His sacrifice is equal to hers, or greater. He loves her unconditionally and shows it sacrificially.

## 3. *Christ loves the Church **redemptively**.*

To redeem means to buy back by the payment of a price. When someone borrows money at a pawn shop, he leaves his watch or stereo or other possession, and has to go back to "redeem" his possession by paying money. If the man does not perform his word, the pawn broker has the right to keep and sell his possession. In a similar way, God watches over His Word to perform it,[14] which means He redeems His Word. When He gives His Word to us, He keeps it, fulfills it and performs it.

The male redeems nothing. He may promise his wife the moon, but she'll only get green cheese. He's promised and broken his promises so many times that she and the children have lost all trust in him. His children don't depend on what he says, then he wonders why they're disobedient and his wife is disrespectful. He can shout scriptures at them, "respect your husband" or "obey your parents," but they don't respond because he hasn't loved them redemptively.

The man intends to keep his word when he gives it. He's sincere, but he's not honest because he doesn't fulfill his promise. When he gives her his word and does not perform it, she still has it. That means he doesn't "keep" it, but she does. Because the culture considers lying acceptable, and professionals such as lawyers are given "license to lie," as one called it, men see nothing wrong with unfulfilled intentions to keep their word.

But the covenant man, a Christlike man, swears to his own hurt and changes not.[15] He loves his wife redemptively and if he gives her a promise, he fulfills it.

These three characteristics, consciously acted upon—unconditional, sacrificial, and redemptive—will build love that is eternal.

## EVIDENCES OF LOVE

Once you love as Christ loves, you'll see the evidence of that God-kind of love in your life.

### 1. Christ's love is selfless.

The Incarnation of God as man was the greatest self-emptying that could ever be.[16]

The male, having never accepted responsibility for his own actions, much less those of others, is patently self-centered and selfish.

The man who does accept responsibility can still be self-centered and adolescent in his attitude toward his family. What concerns him, not them, takes priority in his life. He may appear the good family man with the fine children, but he has limits—and when those limits are reached, divorce is an option. The world is filled with such men—responsible and often hard-working—but selfish. In the Bible this is described as "flesh" ruling the life. This is simple human nature outside of the control of the Holy Spirit.

But the covenant man gives himself for the one loved and loves without thought for self.

*2. Christ's love wants the greatest benefit for the one loved.*

Because of His desire for our benefit, Christ came to earth to make us one with God the Father.

With the male, his personal pleasure comes first. Whatever pleases him is what she has to be satisfied with. He gives no thought to his family's spiritual welfare. He'll go with the "guys" while they go to church, because their eternal destiny is of no concern to him.

The man is concerned with his wife's and family's benefit, if it benefits him as well. His pleasure comes from the benefit he derives from her love. In his perversion of thought, he doesn't consider her receiving benefit from his love.

But the covenant man considers his wife first. She's part of his life, part of his flesh. She's the one bonded to him in marriage and he doesn't just defer to her, but he prefers her. Whatever is necessary for his family's benefit is his daily priority, and he will do whatever necessary to ensure their eternal destiny as well.

*3. Christ's love desires unity.*

Jesus prayed in His high priestly prayer, that we on earth might be "one" even as He and the Father are "One." Our unity with the Father was His priority in life.

The male is content to live with a woman without marrying her because marriage requires commitment. You're only committed to what you confess, and in the absence of the confession of unselfish love in the marriage vows, it's easy for a male to walk away. Having only lived with her and taken the best of her life for his personal pleasure, like a child walking away from its mother, he leaves her. Such males routinely leave the women they impregnate, because their only idea of "unity" is sex, without thought to responsibility for the consequences.

The man does marry, but he lives like he's single. He wants the authority over a wife and children, but not the accountability for it. He resents it when she tries to hold him to account, and blames her for his own infractions. It's a house divided. Life is not easy but hard—hardened through the sin of loving self more than a wife.

The covenant man recognizes that he is one in spirit with her. A covenant partner! Theirs is a house united and therefore it will stand the pressures of adversity and the tests of time. He is committed to a covenant partnership which is not 50-50, but 100-100. He recognizes unity and is committed to seeing greater unity between them. He loves being united with her, sharing together, growing together, and being one in Christ. Theirs is a blessed life.

## PROVISIONS OF LOVE

A covenant man carries out the characteristics of love aggressively, purposefully, and as a result experiences the evidence of that love. Through his love, he makes provisions for his spouse, the same provisions Christ made for believers in the Church.

### 1. Christ gives identity to believers.

Jesus came to be identified with our sin, so that we might become identified with His righteousness. Believers bear Christ's name, Christian. Christ has ensured His Name is a Name which those who follow Him are honored to bear.

The male has an identity crisis—personally, professionally and spiritually. Because he refuses to be responsible for anything, he cannot commit himself to anything, and his unresolved identity crisis makes him a double-minded man, unstable in all his ways.[17] He plays the fool, bouncing from job to job, person to person, relationship to relationship, trying to take care of a problem he has never bothered to identify. His name is not worth much because his word is not worth much, so he cannot provide an identity that a wife would want from a husband.

The man gives his wife a name, but without character. Thinking his personality is sufficient, he fails in marriage because he has majored in externals of charisma and charm, and flunked the internals. When the charm wears off, it's not worth being identified with what little character is found.

The covenant man has a strong identification resolution with himself and with God in Christ. He is able to build his marriage on the good character he has. And he can give his wife an identity with which she is pleased. She is proud to bear his name. He is proud for his wife to bear his name.

## 2. Christ gives believers security.

Jesus Christ doesn't worry. We never have to worry about Him because He's never worried about anything. He is certain of Who He is, what His ministry and mission are, and He is unchanging in His motivations.

The male is insecure in himself and transfers that to his wife. His inferiority, insecurity and indecision gives her little security in their marriage, their relationship or their home life. She decides for them because he won't, then she endures him blaming her for the decisions. She knows she'll work, even when her children are babies, because she never knows what he's going to do, or where he's going to go, and cannot depend on his support.

A man can accept responsibility for his actions, but because he doesn't look to God's Word as the sole source of his conduct, he adopts philosophies from others which are just rationalizations to justify their failures. Worldly wise, yet without wisdom, by accepting others' philosophies, he accepts their failure. He can give his wife a mink coat, but can't offer her security. He generally has a "renter's mentality," willing to rent but not buy, insensitive to his wife's need for a secure home. Like renting, he loves his wife temporarily, not permanently.

The covenant man is the Jehovah Jireh in the marriage, the "Lord Who Provides." He provides his wife security by acting on faith in Christ to meet the needs of his wife and family. He knows their needs because he asks questions and listens to their answers. Because he has developed in his relationship with the Lord, he becomes the problem solver when there is a need in the home. His wife finds security primarily because he is resolute in his commitment to the marriage.

### 3. Christ gives believers stability.

Jesus Christ is the same yesterday, today and forever. There is no variableness or changing in Him. He is the rock for the faith of every believer.

The male is the jock interested in his own pleasure. He is always looking for the big hit. He lives for today, content with this week's check, with no thought or plan for tomorrow. He has no concern for others, but tends to use them for his livelihood. The lottery is his bank, and he has no shame in telling others what he would do if he won it. His wife can believe he'll be there for her about as often as his lottery picks earn him the big win.

The man is filled with self-doubt so he says one thing and lives another. Or he's single-minded, purposeful, deliberate, has goals, plans, ambitions, aspirations and desires, and as a result he's so focused or concentrated on what he wants to do that he has no time for his wife or family. He thinks he's a rock, but those fastened to him find themselves sinking.

The covenant man is single-minded, decisive, honest, steadfast, energetic, and gives his wife stability. She knows where he'll be each day when the sun rises and when the moon comes up. If he travels, he calls her. If he works eight to five, the first thing he does when he comes home is inquire about her welfare. She never has to worry about him changing his mind about marrying her. Because he tells her every day how much he loves her, and matches his words with corresponding actions, she never has a moment's doubt in him or his commitment to her.

## WHAT KIND ARE YOU?

The covenant man's wife has identity, security and stability. What God provides for the Church through Christ, the covenant man provides for his wife because he loves her with a God-kind of love.

The hallmark of the covenant man is his integrity. He knows the character of God and the scripture that says, "Then said the LORD unto me, Thou hast well seen: for I will hasten my word to perform it."[18] Or as the Psalmist reported, that he swears to his own hurt and doesn't change. Because he is Christlike, he realizes that how he reverences his word shows how he reverences God's Word. He is a testimony to truthfulness. His wife can count on him keeping his word. She has confidence that he tells her the truth.

The covenant man lives in the Kingdom of God by faith, and seeks to live in obedience to God's Word, having been brought into a covenant relationship with God through the redemption given him by Christ upon the Cross.

He's the uncommon man, not the average, and definitely not the mediocre male. What kind of a man are you? A male, a mere man or a covenant man?

1 Mark 10:45; Luke 22:27
2 Luke 14:33; Matthew 19:29
3 Mark 7:15
4 Matthew 5:29-30
5 John 13:34
6 Luke 16:20; 14:13; 7:39
7 John 13:1
8 John 8:58
9 Hebrews 13:8
10 Ephesians 5:25
11 Romans 5:5
12 John 13:1
13 Ezekiel 36:26
14 Jeremiah 1:12
15 Jeremiah 1:12; Psalm 15:4
16 Philippians 2:7
17 James 1:8
18 Jeremiah 1:12

# CHAPTER FOURTEEN

# TEN INVESTMENTS YOU MUST MAKE

"How many of you men are fathers?" I ask the crowd of men in the stadium. It looks like a hundred thousand hands are raised.

"How many of you have sons?" The crowd shuffles while some hands go down.

"And how many of you have daughters?" More shuffling and shifting, and still a sea of hands are up.

"Now, how many of you men are more careful about your daughters than you are about your sons?" A ripple of laughter before I make my point. "Because you don't want someone going out with your daughter who is like you used to be."

They explode with laughter, shouts and high fives all around. Then I ask my next question.

"How many of you believe the Bible?" All hands go up.

"How many of you believe the Ten Commandments?" All hands stay raised.

"How many of you can name all ten of them right now?" Very few hands stay up, as men chuckle nervously and glance around to see who bested them. Humorous, but only sadly so, as these questions bring out a point. How can we believe something we don't know? Yet ninety-five percent of all Christian men polled cannot recite the Ten Commandments.

The father's responsibility is to teach his children God's commandments.[1] "Teach to teach to teach" is the principle.[2] But how can we teach something we haven't learned?

God's ten instructions to Moses are contained in what is called the "Decalogue" in the Old Testament, meaning "ten words," or more commonly, "The Ten Commandments." The commandments contain the vision for a civilization to continue in perpetuity throughout generations. Without the commandments, upon which our entire legal system is founded, there is no foundation for a moral society.

The Ten Commandments were never intended to be a means of salvation. They are not a set of regulations to be kept in order to earn our way to heaven through works. Salvation is a free gift of God and cannot be earned. God gave the commandments to Moses after His favor had already been freely given to the nation of Israel, as shown in their miraculous deliverance from the bondage of Egypt.

Obedience to the ten was commanded only for the benefit of God's people, to allow them to live in harmony. Still today, the commands give a people or nation a concrete set of laws, or principles, that provide order. The commandments were the basis for Israel's existence, and our own, as a special people of God, under His divine direction and guidance. Transgression of the commands breaks the law, and gives rise to wars and the criminal element. Obedience brings peace.

## INVEST IN YOUR OWN LIFE!

The commands are ten investments you must make in your life, your career, and especially your marriage if you want the payoff of success, harmony, and a satisfying relationship with your spouse. They are ten tools which you control yourself whereby you can build joy and fulfillment into your own life, regardless of what others do. Obedience to them grants you peace.

This book has been written based on the Ten Commandments, to teach them to you in a practical and relevant way.

After warning you about your own culture, basically all I've taught you in the preceding chapters are the ten. Here they are:[3]

### 1. *"You shall have no other Gods before me."*

Make a decision to serve God first and foremost. God's throne is not a duplex. Because He is our God and Creator, God can demand absolute loyalty, and be righteous in doing so. Everything for a man lands right here on this one choice. It is a forced option. No one can escape this choice. Not choosing is itself a choice.

The Bible says only a fool believes there is no God. Smug "atheists" deny what they instinctively know to be true. As the atheist's son said to him one day, "Dad, do you think God knows we don't believe in Him?"

God alone knows what is best for us, and He alone, even more than we ourselves, is always working toward our highest good. Jesus taught that when we put the kingdom of God first, all other things will be added to us.[4] Men typically put these five before God: provision, pleasure, power, position and popularity. Only when God is first and foremost in our lives will the others give satisfaction, and only then will the rest of the commandments become easy to follow. Jesus said the First Commandment is the greatest, upon which all others rest.

### 2. *"You shall not make for yourself a carved image."*

Avoid the easy traps, the increased idolatry in our culture, not the least of which is pornography.

Idolatry is basically the worship of self. On his way down from the mountain with the tablets containing the commandments, Moses heard a strange sound. Israel had made a golden calf in his absence and were celebrating the new god of their own creation. In his anger at their presumptive sin he broke the tablets. Later Israel would take a piece of wood, and think nothing of burning half for heat and cooking, and use the other half to carve an idol to worship. Stupid! Yet we do the same today, worshiping cars, images and products made with our own hands. We attempt to create a god that conforms to our image, which we believe we can control, but we only become enslaved by sin.

It seems easier to try to make God like us, than to let God make us like Him. But that is actually the hardest road of all. We are not to worship anything but God.

3. *"You shall not take the name of the Lord your God in vain."*

All profanity is based on taking God's Name in vain. To call yourself a "Christian" without corresponding character is taking that Name in vain, which is wrong. "Be right" by building character within yourself, and learn what kind of character you need to become an irresistible husband.

4. *"Remember the Sabbath day to keep it holy."*

The Sabbath proclaims we are not slaves but free men. It is more than a day of rest, it's a day of worship, so rise—wake up!—to worship on that day, and commit yourself to a local church. A church is made strong by your ministry being part of it. A strong church unites your family and makes the community strong.

5. *"Honor your father and mother, that your days may be long on the earth."*

The first four commandments are vertical, dealing with our relationship to God. The last six are horizontal, dealing with our relationship to our fellow man. This is the first commandment with promise, and if you obey it, your life will become "well" in any area of lack.

A child's first introduction to authority is through his parents or surrogate parents. It is easy to trust and believe the Lord if he trusts and believes his parents. If not, he must forgive them, then become a man whose children can trust and believe. Through forgiveness, you can stop the curse from being spread to the next generation.

### 6. *"You shall not murder."*

Whoever harbors anger and hatred against his brother is in danger of God's judgment.[5] You set your own judgment by the words you speak, which come from your heart. Murder begins in the heart from our thoughts and meditations.[6] We can murder a reputation, dreams, faith, or even just ideas. Grace is the antidote to murder. When we deal with people in grace, we set our own judgment according to grace.

### 7. *"You shall not commit adultery."*

Connecting with your wife in intimate relationship is the surest way to avoid falling for the temptation of adultery. Not only do you recognize your desire for intimacy, but you now have the tools whereby it can be accomplished in your life.

Adultery is possible only if people are prepared to hurt others, to enjoy themselves at the expense of others. Adultery is really murder against the covenant of marriage.

### 8. *"You shall not steal."*

Stealing is trespassing on another's right of possession. Because your wife and children have a right to you, you cannot take time which should be invested in them, and spend it elsewhere. To help with this, you now have a 30-step plan for "Daily Living." By concentrating on just one part of that plan each day of the month, and repeating it monthly, you will create a pattern in your life that over the years will give you a strong relationship with your wife, and ensure the love and respect of your children.

9. *"You shall not bear false witness against your neighbor."*

If a person is unwilling to speak ill of another, he is less likely to steal from him or commit murder. To lie is to act like the devil. Your career and marriage cannot be blessed if they are based on a lie, and you cannot have God's blessing on your life if you stand in agreement with Satan rather than Him. Armed with that understanding, you can earn a good living and find favor with God and with man.

10. *"You shall not covet."*

The tenth commandment is an outgrowth of the first. If a person's heart is fixed on God, he will have a right attitude toward others. Your attitude is as the Apostle Paul's, who said, "godliness with contentment is great gain."[7] To be grasping for more, discontent with what you have, idolatrous and lustful in desires, costs you your relationship with God and with your spouse.

## WHY THESE TEN?

God's commandments were chiseled on tablets of stone, not on sand where they would be subject to wind and rain to destroy. They originate from God Himself, from His unchanging and eternal character, so their moral value cannot change. They were given and written by God Himself, therefore not subject to man's changes, amendments, qualifications, or erasures.

Adrian Rogers from Memphis gives seven facts concerning the commandments. The Ten Commandments are:

1 - absolute—not obsolete.
2 - given in perpetuity for each generation.
3 - for a righteous social structure.
4 - given to each individual on which to build character.

5 - given to every family to build a strong family.
6 - guidelines to daily living.
7 - an essential element in God's covenant
with His people.

Jesus did not come to set aside the Ten Commandments, but to establish and fulfill them. No one had ever lived the law in perfection. It was impossible. So until Jesus came in His perfection, it had not been established. He gave the law validity, force and value.

Jesus took the law from being a work of the flesh to a work of the Spirit, making it the basis for a New Covenant with God through Him. His blood shed, and His life given, was the price paid for the new moral law of love to come into effect.

Then Jesus summed up the entire Ten Commandments with: "Do for others what you want them to do for you. This is the teaching of the laws of Moses in a nutshell."[8] What a simple method to ensure a sensational marriage, a stable society and a successful life.

Oddly enough, even though the ten commandments are the basis for a good and godly society, in American culture today, we are not allowed to post them on a post office wall, in a school classroom, or in a business work place. No wonder crime runs rampant! The nation has lost its vision of morality by abandoning God's commandments.

Your generation is the first in America that has never been taught the Ten Commandments, and is not aware that absolute rules exist in the universe. Most men around you do not understand that human behavior is governed by a force set in motion by God, and that working against that force is to work against ourselves. Since only God sees the entire picture of our lives, from birth to death, and because only He can be trusted absolutely to do what is best concerning us, cooperating with His Holy Spirit in obedience to His Word is the only way to ensure a good life for ourselves.

We must engage the Holy Spirit to inscribe the commandments on the tablets of our hearts. Then our consciences have a righteous standard by which to witness our words and actions, whether they are right or not.

## TEACH YOUR CHILDREN WELL

You can reverse today's trend by committing to teach your children the truth as you build your family with your wife. If you don't teach the Ten Commandments to your children, they grow up going to church and hearing about grace, but without the consciousness of sin they never understand the impact that the Cross has on their lives.

When we don't fully understand God's Word, and what is at stake eternally, we don't appreciate the need to be saved. We have no understanding of the spiritual nature of the law, so we continue to live in inward lawlessness with an unchanged heart. Without knowing the law, we never fully appreciate the blessings and comfort of the gospel. People trample underfoot the blood of Christ every day because they do not value His sacrifice. They fail to see the price paid at Calvary. In the absence of understanding, they have no knowledge they're breaking the law and guilty before God. This is why grace is so great, so marvelous, and forgiveness for sin is so rich.

Teaching your children the effect the commandments have had in your own life can build a bridge between your experience and their innocence, and give them a path to live their lives as you have lived yours. One man told me about bringing his whole family together to have communion. For the first time ever, he told them what he'd done as a sinner, how he became saved, and what God's grace had taught him throughout his life.

"Dad, I thought you were just preaching at us all this time," his son said incredulously. "I didn't know you knew what you were talking about."

Our legacy is leaving our testimony with our children of what God has done for us. Children may not always listen to us, but they will always imitate us. They'll never forget the day you passed to them the legacy of your testimony.

Twenty years ago I wrote that the absentee father was the curse of our day. The problem at that time was both the father who didn't live in the home or who sat in front of the television while in the home and didn't interact with the family. Now, twenty years later, the problem is not merely absenteeism, but fatherlessness, which is the absence of concern for a man's children. It is a problem which I have witnessed worldwide. In African nations, I've seen soldiers who were just 14 and 15 years old. Over a half-million parentless children are said to be roaming the streets of Zimbabwe today because of the AIDS virus wiping out the adult population.

Fatherless children have no knowledge of right or wrong behavior. They cannot recognize it in others, nor can they see it in themselves. They're completely mystified when they are arrested or looked down upon, because they believe they're living the best way they can, and shouldn't be blamed for it. "The character of our children is the leading indicator of the future of our country," said Senator Dan Coats of Indiana. Yet we have just raised the first generation of fatherless children.

God said His commandments were to be taught by fathers to children who would teach their children.[9] *A father's responsibility to his children is to teach them the Ten Commandments*. If he loves them, he will instruct them.

"For he established a testimony in Jacob, and appointed a law in Israel, which he commanded our fathers, that they should make them known to their children: That the generation to come might know them, even the children which should be born; who should arise and declare them to their children: That they might set their hope in God, and not forget the works of God, but keep his commandments."[10]

In America we have seen battles ensue on the issue of taking the Ten Commandments off a courthouse wall, yet in most homes, even Christian homes, the parents have not posted the Ten Commandments for their own children. Which is the greater sin? Post the commandments conspicuously in your home, even in the children's bedrooms or bathrooms. Be a wise man and give them a rock to build upon as Jesus instructed us, rather than the shifting sands of vagrant philosophies.

The irresistible husband as a strong father, instructing his children in the way of righteousness, is a glory to his family, and a wonder to his wife, which makes him "wonderful." Unwise men who ignore truth pale by comparison.

[1] Deuteronomy 6
[2] II Timothy 2:2
[3] Exodus 20:1-17
[4] Matthew 6:33
[5] Matthew 5:21
[6] Matthew 15:19; Mark 7:21
[7] I Timothy 6:6
[8] Matthew 7:12
[9] Deuteronomy 6:1
[10] Psalm 78:5-7

## CHAPTER FIFTEEN

# STAND UP AND FIGHT!

And the list goes on! Another influential leader declared he and his wife are getting a divorce. Still another international minister is openly talking about divorcing his wife. Both of them are shockers! An epidemic? Or worse—a plague? Why do men pursue known wickedness?

Has the doctrine of Jehovah being a "God of the second chance" taken hold of the Christian mindset as a justification for personal preference? Do Christians listen to hip hop lyrics about killing a wife that's not liked anymore, and figure they're not that bad when all they do is divorce her instead? Do they watch Schwarzeneggar say, "Consider this a divorce," and blow his movie wife's head off and think, "well, at least I just killed the marriage in court?"

Where are all the *men* these days? Where are the covenant men who know how to keep their word? Who value the love of a wife? Who will fight for the honor of God?

It seems to me, from lyrics that have become popular, to the invention of Internet "dating," to the rise of every sort of social ill, that our nation has collectively raised a bumper crop of weak-willed males who want the easy way or no way at all. One man I know divorced his wife because she spent too much money. Too much money? What does he think divorce and child support will cost him for the next eighteen years? Not to mention the mental torture his child will undergo for years because of both parents' selfishness.

Close to half of all young people getting married today are products of broken homes. Do they really want to inflict on their children what was done to them? Or do they change their memories when the going gets tough and say, "it wasn't that hard for me, my kids will make it." How selfish to choose a hard road for your children instead of taking the hard road yourself!

## HARD HEARTS AND HARD HEADS

Jesus said the only reason God gave divorce through Moses was because of "hardness of heart." Have we so eviscerated the Bible by theological surgery that we have excised what we do not want to obey? Do we read, "God hates divorce,"[1] then say, "yeah, but He allowed it," as if one negates the other? That's a hard-hearted viewpoint. It shows a hard head, too.

Any spouse who rejects reason, truth and reality can become hard-hearted. The Pharisees' hardness of heart occurred because "they saw in Jesus that which they disapproved."[2] Jesus dined with those they rejected, ministered to those they denied, and loved those they hated. Jesus called the Pharisees "vipers"—cunning, malignant, wicked men. Religious? Yes. Rebellious? YES! Hard of heart? Absolutely.

One men's ministry conducted a survey of those who attended their meetings and found that almost 50% of the men did not believe that Bible truth was absolute. In other words, truth was relative to our circumstances. Liberal theologians would love those men.

By such standards:
- taking a life is justifiable
- truth is relative
- holiness is archaic
- church is seasonal
- obedience is optional
- marriage is conditional
- ministers are exceptions
- absolutes have become provisional

Has the Bible simply become a source of motivational maxims? Is it merely a quote book for political candidates? Is salvation now only necessary for faith to obtain material possessions? When did "dysfunctional" replace "sin" in our glossary?

Our churches reflect the softness of our spirits. A pastor I know conducts "Church Express"—in 'n' out in forty-five minutes. Today we have fifteen-year veterans of Christianity sitting in the pew settling for a good lifestyle while hundreds of thousands of teens are studying the "martyrs" because they expect they may be the next one.

The Apostle Paul wrote, "Having begun in the Spirit are we now made perfect in the flesh?"[3] The flesh can make nothing perfect because it is imperfect at best and will never be anything but a source of death to the life of Christ within us. *The flesh will always conspire with the world to betray us into the hands of the devil.*

We are deceived when we think we are above obedience to God's Word. His law is perfect and leads to life. It is foolish senselessness, and invalidates the whole reason for Christ's coming, for us to believe we can live by our own desires at the expense of God's Word. Insane.

The Cross was our only means of being accepted by the Father in Heaven. We need Jesus to save us! Most of all we need to be saved from ourselves—our decisions—our passions—our willfulness—our deception. We need Jesus to save us from walking in the flesh, to enable us to walk in His Spirit, which leads to life and peace. His Spirit will never lead us to do what is contrary to the will, way and Word of God.

## THERE IS NO REASON TO EXPLORE EVIL

Are you going to consider divorce?

Only the hard-hearted would think it made sense to defy

God and seek evil. All knowledge binds. The knowledge of evil destroys power and imposes slavery. It is an awful hour when we first feel the need to hide something evil we've done or linked ourselves to. Hiding anything makes your whole life different. Questions are feared, eyes are avoided, subjects cannot be touched, the zest and sparkle of innocence is lost, mental freedom passes into slavery, and the mind and emotion bear the marks of its tyranny.

Men cannot will to forget. Thinking evil to be exciting or exotic, men are deceived into pollution and contamination that can only be erased by the Word of God and Blood of Christ. Someone said, "I appreciate being a Christian more because of what I went through before I was saved." Nonsense! The response to such a statement is a question: "Would the Temple have been lovelier because it had once been a brothel?"

The Apostle Paul addressed this mentality when he said, "Shall we continue in sin that grace may abound—God forbid. How can we that are dead to sin live any longer therein?"[4]

We live in the world but we are not of the world. The "world" is the earth with its inhabitants, the human race and specifically the whole mass of men alienated from God, and therefore hostile to the cause of Christ. Worldly affairs, the aggregate of things earthly, the whole circle of earthly goods, endowments, riches, advantages, pleasures, are hollow and frail and fleeting, yet stir desire, seduce from God and are obstacles to the cause of Christ in your life and the life of your family. People excuse away their evil actions with "everybody does it."

No reason under the heavens exists for you to entertain thoughts that would dishonor your wife, God, His Word— or your word. A friend of mine told his wife when he divorced her, "Well I guess this is the way I am, so I'll just go with it."

He's leaving Christ to go with what? Another woman who is jaded, lewd and a lover of sin? What about Christ's sacrifice for him? Where is the Cross? Isn't Jesus real? Doesn't Jesus live in the heart? How can a person simply tell himself Jesus doesn't count? Where is the fear of the Lord?

Is Hell a destination of choice? Where is the consciousness of evil or righteousness? How can a man simply turn his back on a precious salvation and count it as worthless, in order to indulge in lewdness?

## ARE YOU UP TO THE FIGHT?

Living the Christ-life is not necessarily simple and is sometimes out-and-out hard. Yet there is no harder road in the long run than the road of sin. When all is said and done, no life is easier than to have stayed married to the same woman for over 50 years. Nothing is harder than divorcing once, twice, three times.

I cannot understand men who have the opportunity to stand for truth yet become passive, compliant and acquiescent. Why give in when faced with a divorce plague that is taking its toll on even those who seem stable and spiritual? This is not a time to sit idly by and watch Satan picking off God's people. This is a time for real manhood. *Stand up and fight*!

"There are times when real manhood rebels against easygoing tolerance and soft indulgence and promiscuous assent, and despises moderation and inaction," writes Dr. Speer in his book, "The Marks of a Man."

Where is the man who wants to stand against unrighteousness and evil? Let him show it so the whole world can see.

Are men so afraid of sin, Satan or self that they can no longer fight for God, good and family? When Eliab, King David's eldest brother, saw David at the battle line against the enemy he rebuked David for being there.

"And Eliab his eldest brother heard when he spake unto the men; and Eliab's anger was kindled against David, and he said, Why camest thou down hither? and with whom hast thou left those few sheep in the wilderness? I know thy pride, and the naughtiness of thine heart; for thou art come down that thou mightest see the battle. And David said, What have I now done? Is there not a cause?"[5]

David's brother, out of jealousy, tried to convince David there was no cause for which to fight. For us today, is there not a cause? There is! The same cause as David's—it's a fight for the honor of God! But where are the men who will fight?

Goliath the Giant challenged the armies of Israel to fight. None dared but David. He fought the worthy cause. He won a noble fight. To him came the esteem of men, the tight relationship with God, and a future filled with the promises of God.

In a later era, Daniel had the courage and boldness in the face of cultural adversity to throw open his window and pray—even though the lions' den would be his reward. Daniel's was a lawbreaking of civil disobedience.[6] When civil law demands a violating or breaking of God's law—God's law is obeyed.

John the Baptist preached in the wilderness and thousands of people made the arduous trek out to hear him. His beheading illustrates to this day that some things in life are more important than life itself.

Moses, as an adult, refused to be called the son of Pharaoh's daughter; choosing rather to be afflicted along with the people of God, than to enjoy the pleasures of the sin of his culture. He esteemed the reproach of Christ as greater riches than the treasures of Egypt, for he had respect for the reward God would give him for his stand.[7]

When David killed Goliath, the people sang his praises. When a man stands up for what it right and overcomes the enemies of his and God's, people still sing his praises. Who will sing yours? The wife you divorce or the one you stay true to for a lifetime?

There is no reason to run to evil, and every reason to avoid it. The following is a pertinent, patient, poignant letter written by a girl to a father who caved in to the dictates of the culture around him and turned her childhood home into a house of horror:

## A Wish For A Father

Dear Fathers:

I am a 13-year-old girl who attends church where some of the men are having problems with their marriages, and some are thinking of divorce. If you are a father thinking about leaving your family, I don't believe you truly know in your heart what your child is (or children are) going through. My parents are divorced, and this is my thought from a kid's point of view.

I may seem to many as a normal 13-year-old girl. I smile on the outside and show a positive and happy attitude, but inside I am crying out so loud for a "normal" family life. You see, my father left my mom when I was 18 months old. Oh sure, he probably thought that I was too young for the divorce to affect me, but, oh, how wrong he was!

What happened to the commitment, the promise, that he made to my mom, and most importantly, to God? How could he have ever made such a selfish decision to leave us? Did he ever think how his decision affected so many lives? Will he ever understand what I'm feeling, and will he ever realize he has scarred me for life?

I just want to be a normal kid. What is so wrong with that? I've sat in restaurants for the last 10 years, staring at the complete families around us, wondering what it would be like to have a father at home, to have a father kiss me goodnight and listen to my prayers. A father to be there at my volleyball and basketball games, to look at my report cards, meet my teachers, or maybe even tell me, "I love you." But all the waitress sees is the smile on my face. Doesn't my dad know how much he has hurt me?

If God gave me one wish, and one wish only, I would wish for my father to watch me grow up. Every Christmas he sends me presents that a child would play with. He buys me stuffed animals and clothes that only a five year old would wear. I think he still pictures me as a little kid, and always will. He wasn't there when I had my birthdays. He wasn't there for my school events, or my girl scout awards programs. He never met any of my teachers and never saw a report card. It was always my mom and my grandparents that showed me that they loved me so much they would do anything in order to make me happy.

I'm sure my dad thought 10 years ago when he made the decision to leave, that he could still be a good father and be there for me anytime. Well, things change through time. He started out seeing me once a week, then every other weekend. Then he moved to another state. I've only seen him once since then. Phone calls are seldom. Did he realize our father-daughter relationship would end like this?

I guess you can say that my mom was, well, my mom and dad rolled into one. I think the divorce was kind of hard for her, and still is, but she handles it so well. She tries to make up for me not having a father around and doesn't have time to go out and possibly meet a new husband. She works 2 jobs and we have our own home now. I don't think she makes a lot of money, but somehow we make it OK. God is definitely with us.

She makes sure that I go to a good school and a good church. She goes to most of my school activities and takes off work to go to my volleyball and basketball tournaments. She has also done the "father" things, such as taking me camping and she was even an assistant basketball coach last year at the YMCA. She thinks of me before she even has a thought about herself, which is so much more than what my dad would give me.

Sometimes, I just think of my father as a friend because he doesn't act like a true father. I bet that my father doesn't even know what "father" means. And if he does, well he is not the type of person I would call a father. The word—father—means to me someone that could keep a commitment, not only with his wife, but with his child or children also. I think that this word also means that someone loves you, cares for you, and doesn't lie to you about anything.

I find myself saying that I really love him, but deep inside, I feel that after all that he has done to me, he is just another human being. I know this is an awful thing to say, but what do you expect me to say? He leaves me and my mom in a not so good position financially, scars a child's life so bad that she can't forgive him, and you expect me to just say, oh, that's OK? I think NOT!!!

These past couple of years, I guess you could say that I haven't really been myself. When I go to school and someone brings up the subject of fathers, I just freeze and think what it would be like even to have a father around the house. When my friends talk about their dads right in front of me, I just kind of close the subject out, try to avoid it, and then go somewhere else.

You may be thinking that this won't happen if you get a divorce. Well, here's a tip for you—you are not a child, you do not know what a child is going through. You don't know what your child is feeling or even thinking … and you most likely will never hear another 13 year old express her inside feelings with a stranger. All of these years I have been just keeping this whole thing, and all of my feelings, to myself. So if you want advice and you want to know what your child is feeling, you should really, really, strongly consider what all I have said.

My father got what he wanted. He couldn't face the responsibility for me. He got his freedom. He dated lots of girls, lived with them, even married the last one when he got her pregnant. I just hope my dad is happy now after all that he has done. Well, my father thought the divorce would make him happy, but what it boils down to is—he just wasn't happy with himself. He gambled and what he didn't realize is that he has lost his little girl.

If you are thinking about getting a divorce, think hard. Not only is God crying with sadness, but so are your children. Being a good "off-site" father is impossible. Be strong and be the husband and father you promised to be. If being a father is important to you, then stick with your marriage.

Think of your kids. We are crying for your love and fulfilled promises.

## The Horror Of Divorce!

One day years ago, after counseling a couple who were in the throes of deciding on a divorce, I realized my love for my wife Nancy and desire for her welfare were an overpowering affection against such a thing. I sat down and wrote these words to her, impassioned by the moment, but never given to her. I forgot even writing it for many years until I found the letter after our 50th wedding anniversary.

Divorce! The very word strikes terror to my heart, sends shudders of fear down my spine far worse than even the word cancer.

I cannot conceive of another man holding you in a loving embrace, touching your lips growing soft, tender and sweet with loving passion. Or to think of someone else putting their hand on the places sacred to our marriage.

It is utterly horrible to imagine him sitting at the breakfast table with our children, listening to them tell of what they are going to do that day with their childish enthusiasm. Missing the looks on their faces, shining with the drowsy delight of waking to another day filled with the mercies of God.

The sight of another than me having the wonder of watching you prepare for bedtime. Or the sight and sound of your daily wonder—preparing a meal, talking to the children, watching television, and talking on the phone all at the same time.

If I never told you I loved you enough, did enough to prove it, gave enough of myself to you, then please forgive me. Sometimes I became engrossed in what I was doing, failed to pay attention to you, and I regret every selfish moment of my life with you.

I am frightened at the prospect of being single. Of not knowing how to take care of myself after you have done it with such total caring for so long. I'm not sure I could make that adjustment, and I know I wouldn't be able to make wise decisions without your advice and counsel.

The thought of dating is anathema to me. It seems so vulgar somehow, and a violation of my very nature to attempt to find someone else to love. No! There is no place to go to find again what I had that is now so precious and priceless. There will never be a replacement for you—never. You are the original, all others would simply be an attempt to have a copy.

1   Malachi 2:16
2   Luke 15:2
3   Galatians 3:3
4   Romans 6:1-2
5   1 Samuel 17:22-29
6   Daniel 6:10
7   Hebrews 11:24-26

## CHAPTER SIXTEEN

# LIVE WITHOUT REGRETS

The hardest thing for a man to take is rejection. The hardest thing for a man to admit is that he is wrong.

Some men would rather divorce than admit their error. They'll let their marriages die because they don't want to go to the Cross, admit their errors, and be purified from wrongdoing. Their "friends" will come along and tell them, "Yeah, that's right, Man, we agree, you're better off without her." And the deed is done, and he's soon alone and lonely, and no better off because he's still the same ole guy doing the same ole thing.

My question is, why listen to losers?

The answer for reconciliation when conflicts arise is to take your problems to the cross! Going to the cross means we die to the flesh so we can live in the Spirit and do the will of the Father even at the expense of ourselves. Taking it to the cross means we'd rather live in the will of God than by the works of the flesh. At the Cross, our old nature has to die and we adopt the new nature of Christ which causes us to please God.

Repentance is necessary to the saving of a soul or of a marriage. God doesn't want apologies, nor does He put band aids on wounds of the heart. He wants genuine repentance. "Repent" is the first word of the gospel message. Repentance rids us of deceit and guilt. It cleanses the heart and the relationship. It leads to reconciliation, restoration and restitution.

Repentance brings grace into action.

God's favor is a manifestation of His grace. "You are their strength. What glory! Our power is based on your favor!"[1]

## A "No Regret" Lifestyle!

Rick had been in the Harvard MBA program where the divorce rate was 75%. Samantha had meted out grace to him, but received little in return as he worked night and day trying to complete his career and provide for his family. She worked and took care of the house, and the entire responsibility of raising the children fell to her. One day, Rick decided to take the time to attend a men's meeting our ministry held nearby.

Samantha will never forget that day because when Rick came home, he stopped her as she mopped the kitchen floor, took the mop out of her hand, poured a large bowl of water, sat her down, then knelt on the kitchen floor in front of her, and asked her to forgive him for taking her for granted, for not ministering to her, and for being absent in leading the family. Then he washed her feet as a symbol of his repentance.

For the next several years, Rick and Samantha ministered to other couples, winning many to Christ and saving many from the heartache of divorce. Then came the awful day that Samantha heard a doctor's report that Rick would need surgery for a mild cancer. They prayed and had a calm assurance that everything would be okay. But after undergoing surgery successfully, in recovery, Rick took a turn for the worse and his young, brilliant earthly life was gone within days.

Samantha told me, "It was important to us in our marriage to live with no regrets. That was the theme of our marriage from the day of our big change until the day Rick died. And I can honestly say, I have no regrets. Our marriage was rich, it touched others, and the foundation he gave to our three small children has lasted even to the present day."

I've heard it said, no man on his deathbed regrets that he didn't spend more time at the office. Our only true regrets are our relationships.

## GIVE GRACE!

How many times do spouses want to quit, forget it all, start over again with someone else? But we have the power to repent, and offer the grace of Jesus Christ. Is today the day for you to take action?

Mark and Pam sat across the table from me and began to recount their journey in marriage and faith. For nine years they had what could be called a good marriage, a comfortable living, and all the externals that beget happiness. Then things began to go wrong with the business, stress settled in, and a year later they were talking divorce.

Finally Mark couldn't take it any longer and started talking to Pam. Months later, they sat across a table from me and recounted their journey.

"I went to Pam and confessed everything—my desire for another woman, my unhappiness with her attitudes. It crushed her. She didn't know what to do, and I didn't either. Pam heard a radio announcement of a meeting and we went. There, we heard what we'd never heard before, and met people who sat up almost all night counseling us. We prayed the prayer of forgiveness. It was hard, but she forgave me. I forgave her. When we left, we were determined to make the marriage work.

"We began to read the Bible together, pray, and talk to each other without fighting. Then I heard about foot washing. So one night a few weeks ago I took the children to a friend's, and lit all the candles in the house before she came home. When she arrived, I knelt in front of her and washed her feet, telling her how much I loved her and how grateful I was to be married to her. Then she washed my feet. We took communion over our bed, in front of the television and VCR, and when we went to bed it was as if we had a new marriage.

"We awoke to find it was still evening, and we were so happy we didn't know how to express it. Even the dog seemed relieved, so we took him for a walk, strolling hand-in-hand through the neighborhood. It was the greatest night of our lives."

Pam eagerly added to Mark's story, "You cannot believe the way I love him now. It's as if I have a new husband who genuinely and truly loves me. Always before there was something missing. I knew it, but I didn't know what to do. When he knelt to wash my feet, it seemed the Holy Spirit was washing my mind, healing my spirit and giving me a new heart. Neither of us have any shame or guilt. It is wonderful."

## GO TO THE CROSS!

The story of redemption finds its center in Christ, whose Cross becomes its symbol. The Cross was eternally in God's mind and heart before it was ever manifested. The Cross, once it bore the blood and broken body of our Lord, became the place of exchange for all of mankind.

At the Cross, we exchange guilt for acquittal. Repentance for faith. Sorrow for joy. Sin for righteousness. Ignorance for eternal knowledge. Disease for healing. Being lost for being found. Homelessness for living in the Father's House. Fatherlessness for a Father's love. Old life for a new creation. Impotence for power. Stupidity for wisdom.

Jesus submitted to the Cross because of man's depravity. We need God's grace through Christ. In and of ourselves, we're incapable of achieving any form of righteousness. If we were capable of any righteousness at all, Jesus would not have had to go to the Cross.

Two trees are pivotal in all of human creation. One tree in the Garden of Eden brought sin and death when man eternally erred. One tree upon which our Savior hung brought righteousness and life when Christ paid for our error.

1.    The Cross is the place of reconciliation—for your marriage, your family.[2]

2 The Cross is where the debt of sin was canceled.

3 The Cross is where Christ triumphed over principalities and powers that were arrayed against us.[3]

4. The Cross is where we have been crucified to the world—and the world crucified to us.[4] "Life Enhancement Christians" have never been to Cross, so they are happy to live in the world and in the church without compunction. With no repentance that leads to faith, we have only presumption.

5. The Cross is where sin is made ineffective and inactive in our bodies, so we no longer live as slaves of sin in the flesh.[5]

In the Passover Celebration, Israel looked back to Egypt and deliverance. In the Christian Communion, we look back to sin and deliverance. God says, "Remember what you used to be. Remember what I did for you. Remember how I did it." It's all by the Blood of the Lamb.[6]

The Cross is God's display of love for the world.[7] To tell of God's love without telling of the Cross is to omit the manifestation of God's love from people, which is error. Only through the Cross can we escape from the wrath of God to come.

God's wrath is settled in regard to sin and has never been seen on the world as it will one day be seen against sin. God's wrath is always regarded in the Scripture as the just, proper, and natural expression of His holiness and righteousness which must always, under all circumstances, and at all costs, be maintained. It is therefore a righteous indignation and compatible with the holy and righteous nature of God.[8]

Why listen to losers? To them, God's wrath is a contradiction against His love. They don't get the Cross because they don't want to get it. To get it would mean they'd have to change to live according to what they really believe in their hearts to be true. Theirs is the worst kind of hypocrisy because if they have a breath before they die, they'll try to "make their peace with God," and even knowing that, they'll live their entire lives as if there were no God.

## FAITH TO THE DEATH

The cross is so pivotal, so crucial, so important, that Satan tempted Jesus to come down from the Cross.[9] By enduring it, Jesus identified with the worst of humanity. For Christ to come down would have left redemption undone. To come down would have given the devil the victory. To come down would have negated the victory Christ won on the Mount of Temptation.

To come down would not have been an act of faith. Job spoke of this kind of faith to the death when he said, *"Though he slay me, yet will I trust him."*[10] To come down would have been worse than going through it. To come down would have violated Christ's nature. To come down would have put the Father to an open shame. To come down would have meant that Christ started in the Spirit but finished in the flesh.[11]

To omit the Cross is to make Christianity no different from any other religion in the world. We take up our cross daily and follow Jesus, doing the will of God at the expense of self, reckoning self dead to do the will of God.

Without the Cross, men can experience reformation, but not resurrection. The Cross is the key to the entire Word of God, which is the key to the entire universe in which we live. All of Scripture points to, reflects back, and centers on this one event. The Cross is the only place where a man can enter the kingdom of God. The Cross is the only place possible where we can appropriate, and appreciate, God's promises.

Without the Cross, we are left alone to try to lift ourselves into the presence of God. With the Cross, the mysteries of revelation are made known to us.

Why listen to losers? Satan will try anything, use anyone, to try to keep you from going to the Cross for your solutions. He calls God a liar.[12] He tries to convince you that your righteousness—or state of being right—is better than Jesus Christ's. He tries to convince you that the pleasure he offers is greater than the pleasing lifestyle we find at the Cross.

To Gentiles at the time of Christ, the Cross was foolishness because without the law, they have no knowledge of sin.[13] "All have sinned and come short of the Glory of God." "There is none righteous, no not one." "Ye must be born again."[14] Man is formed and fashioned in the image of God in darkness and water to be birthed to live in air and light, which is a natural conversion. We were formed and fashioned in darkness and sin to be birthed to live righteousness and light, which is a supernatural conversion. When we're born again, we're born as a new creation in Christ Jesus.

## DIG YOUR WELLS!

God pleads with us now that we've been to the Cross not to harden our hearts as did the children of Israel, who died in the wilderness. *Why let our marriages, careers, businesses, ministries, and children be destroyed when we can live a life without regrets.*

To face harsh realities about ourselves, repent of lusts and unbridled sexual appetites, bring freshness into our lives and families, we can get alone with God until He blasts apart and digs out the stony matter from our hearts. Our Lord Jesus told of a well that contained "living" water. "But whosoever drinketh of the water that I shall give him shall never thirst;

but the water that I shall give him shall be in him a well of water springing up into everlasting life."[15]

The Old Testament is filled with examples for us, types and shadows that point us to the work Christ would do centuries later. The wells dug by men of God back then teach lessons about the spiritual wells we dig in our new covenant with Christ.

In the Old Testament, Isaac prospered as the blessings of God overtook him until it was necessary to provide more water for his growing population of flocks and herds, and the people who cared for them. "For all the wells which his father's servants had digged in the days of Abraham his father, the Philistines had stopped them, and filled them with earth."[16] The wells his father Abraham had dug in his day were now stopped up with debris, rocks and rubbish. Isaac had to clean out the wells so the water could flow freely again.

In the same way that Isaac found his well filled with rubbish, that well of life within us can also become filled with rubbish and in need of cleaning to let the water of life flow freely. Rubbish can be harsh words spoken, impatience with your children, a critical remark to your wife, attitudes that are non-productive and negative, places you've gone or images you've exposed your mind to which need to be obscured by the Cross.

Digging out the rubbish and rocks is not easy, but essential and critical to sustain the growth God is giving us. Isaac found that to embrace the added blessings of a wife, career, children, ministry, and everything else He was given, he had to clear out the wells he'd inherited from his ancestor.

I was walking the beach alone last year, crying out to God for His will in my life, when the Holy Spirit led me to dig some rocks out of the springs in my spirit. God brought up the issues in my life and His Spirit helped me reject them and submit them to the Cross for cleansing. It all had to come out. Then came the glorious moment when I began to praise God, for purity, cleanness, holiness, goodness, and the flow of Christ's living water from the wells of salvation in my spirit became again a rushing mighty flood of the Holy Spirit and anointing. It seemed as if I could run through a fire or leap over a building.

*How wonderful to have a free flowing well of salvation in the heart!*

"The sacrifices of God are a broken spirit: a broken and a contrite heart, O God, thou wilt not despise."[17] King David wrote those words in his penitential Psalm as he cleared the rocks from his heart after committing adultery with Bathsheba.

God has pleasure in those who fear Him. He takes pleasure in those who obey Him. Even when we do some stupid, asinine, sinful, dumb thing, and bring condemnation on ourselves, it is still possible to please God with our godly sorrow and genuine repentance. God is a good God. He loves us even when we do not love ourselves enough to do right. God is love and His grace is always sufficient. "It is His good pleasure to give us the kingdom."[18]

The man who believes on, trusts in and commits his life to Jesus Christ is not a willing partaker of the sinful elements in the culture to which he is born. Rather he finds God's good pleasure in his life by reveling in the culture Christ has provided through the Cross. Because he honors God and applies the truths of God's Word, he lives with inner peace, his home is a place of harmony, love and grace, his children revere him, and to his wife he is truly irresistible.

[1]  Psalm 89:17 TLB
[2]  Ephesians 2:13-16; II Corinthians 5:18-20; Romans 5:9-10
[3]  Colossians 2:13-15
[4]  Galatians 2:20; 6:14
[5]  Romans 6:13-18
[6]  Hebrews 9:22

[7] John 3:16; 15:13; I John 4:10; Romans 5:6-10
[8] John 3:36; Romans 1:18; 2:5; 2:8; Ephesians 2:1-5
[9] Matthew 27:39; Mark 15:29
[10] Job 13:15
[11] Galatians 3:4
[12] I John 5:10
[13] Galatians 3:19-25
[14] John 3:3
[15] John 4:13-14
[16] Genesis 26:15
[17] Psalm 51:17
[18] Luke 12:32

# THE TEN COMMANDMENTS

The Ten Commandments are not a means of salvation, nor regulations to ensure your way to heaven. They are God's means to govern human behavior, a force set in motion by God which working against is to work against ourselves.

Post the commandments conspicuously in your home, even in the children's bedrooms or bathrooms. Be a wise man and give them a rock to build upon as Jesus instructed us, rather than the shifting sands of vagrant philosophies. The father's responsibility is to teach his children God's commandments.

1. Thou shalt have no other gods before me.

2. Thou shalt not make unto thee any graven image.

3. Thou shalt not take the name of the Lord thy God in vain.

4. Remember the sabbath day, to keep it holy.

5. Honour thy father and thy mother.

6. Thou shalt not kill.

7. Thou shalt not commit adultery.

8. Thou shalt not steal.

9. Thou shalt not bear false witness against thy neighbour.

10. Thou shalt not covet.

# Guide To Daily Living

This 30-day planner allows you to concentrate on one item each day of the month to increase stewardship of your family's love and your responsibility to them. Each day, make movement forward in the area listed, and use the entire planner to devote yourself to prayer whenever there is a 31st day. By applying truth over days and months, you will create a pattern in your life that will earn you the respect of your children and ensure the love of your wife.

| Day | Action Item |
|---|---|
| 1 | Set your personal calendar before your business calendar. |
| 2 | Try never to cancel family plans. |
| 3 | Do not let your business, ministry or hobby become an idol, mistress or an excuse. |
| 4 | Do not make your secretary or female colleague an "office wife." |
| 5 | Take periodic honeymoons. |
| 6 | Have regularly scheduled times together. |
| 7 | Keep your personal devotional life vital. |
| 8 | Pray with your wife. |
| 9 | Relationship precedes ministry. Your ministry is only as effective as the relationship you have with your wife. |
| 10 | Give your wife and family love and value. |
| 11 | Don't make your wife a beggar, an employee or an appendage. |
| 12 | Don't make your wife a scapegoat. |

| Day | Action Item |
|-----|-------------|
| 13 | Set times for family council. |
| 14 | Children are not responsible for their parents' problems. |
| 15 | Knowledge requires responsibility. Don't make others responsible for how you feel. |
| 16 | Try never to disagree in front of the children. |
| 17 | Don't make your children an example to other kids. |
| 18 | Both you and your wife continue your education. |
| 19 | Recreation is vital to inspiration. |
| 20 | Make your home your castle. |
| 21 | Help her organize her home. |
| 22 | Don't second-guess your wife publicly. |
| 23 | If spouses travel, they want to be conquering heroes when they come home. |
| 24 | Work with what you have to get what you want. "Despise not the day of small beginnings." |
| 25 | Discipline yourself before you try to discipline others. |
| 26 | You cannot correct in others what is wrong in your own life. |
| 27 | You're a poor specimen if you cannot stand the pressure of adversity. |
| 28 | Ladies, minister to your husband sexually - it's your strength. |
| 29 | Don't try to make your spouse into the image you had of what you wanted to marry. |
| 30 | Communicate. Communicate. Communicate. |

# Nancy Corbett Cole Charities

A portion of the proceeds from this book will be given to Nancy Corbett Cole Charities, serving the abused, addicted and abandoned. Internationally, "Nancy Corbett Cole Homes of Refuge" provide housing, vocational training and education for abused women and children. In the United States, help is ongoing on an individual and corporate basis.

Nancy Corbett Cole, "The Loveliest Lady in the Land," supported her husband, Edwin Louis Cole, in pursuing his life's mission for 54 years. Behind the scenes, she was a spiritual anchor and provider for many. Before her death in December, 2000, Nancy asked for the assurance that those for whom she had provided would not feel her absence. To fulfill that end, and for that purpose, Nancy Corbett Cole Charities were established.

By purchasing this book, you have already helped society's under-served and less priveleged members. If this book helped you, please consider sending a generous donation as well. Your one-time or continual support will help the helpless, heal the hurting, and relieve the needy. Your gift is fully tax-deductible in the U.S. Send your compassionate contribution to:

Nancy Corbett Cole Charities
P.O. Box 92501
Southlake, TX 76092
USA

Thank you for your cheerful and unselfish care for others.

Watch for More Watercolor Books™

by terrific authors like:

Edwin Louis Cole
Nancy Corbett Cole
Donald Ostrom

Many more!


www.watercolorbooks.com


For international orders
or publishing, contact
Access Sales International
www.access-sales.com
or
dianae@access-sales.com

Also by Edwin Louis Cole

*Maximized Manhood*

*Potential Principle*

*Real Man*

*Strong Men in Tough Times*

*ManPower*

*Absolute Answers to Prodigal Problems*

COURAGE

*Communication, Sex & Money*

*Winners Are Not Those Who Never Fail,
but Those Who Never Quit*

*Unique Woman*

TREASURE